PSYCHIC REIKI

PSYCHIC REIKI
Divine Life-Force Energy Healing

BRETT BEVELL

Monkfish Book Publishing Company
Rhinebeck, New York

Psychic Reiki: Divine Life-Force Energy Healing © 2018 by Brett Bevell

Book and cover design by Colin Rolfe
Cover art by Mary DeLave (MaryDeLave.com)

Paperback ISBN: 978-1-939681-84-3
eBook ISBN: 978-1-939681-85-0

Library of Congress Cataloging-in-Publication Data

Names: Bevell, Brett, author.
Title: Psychic reiki : divine life-force energy healing / by Brett Bevell.
Description: Rhinebeck, New York : Monkfish Book Publishing Company, [2018]
Identifiers: LCCN 2018000041 (print) | LCCN 2017061362 (ebook) | ISBN 9781939681850 (ebook) | ISBN 9781939681843 (pbk. : alk. paper)
Subjects: | MESH: Spiritual Therapies | Qi
Classification: LCC RZ403.R45 (print) | LCC RZ403.R45 (ebook) | NLM WB 885 |
   DDC 615.8/52--dc23
LC record available at https://lccn.loc.gov/2018000041

Monkfish Book Publishing Company
22 East Market Street, Suite 304
Rhinebeck, New York 12572
(845) 876-4861
www.monkfishpublishing.com

I dedicate this book to Amma and Neem Karoli Baba for inspiring this work! And to my loving wife Helema, who leaps into my heart every time I think of her! And to my dear son Dylan, the little wizard who fills my life with the magic of love!

Table of Contents

Acknowledgements IX

Introduction XI

Chapter One: What Is Psychic Reiki? 1

Chapter Two: The Psychic Reiki Initiation. 10

Chapter Three: Opening Your Heart to the Divine . . 15

Chapter Four: Psychic Reiki Self Session 21

Chapter Five: Psychic Reiki Session for Another Person . . 25

Chapter Six: Reiki Meditation Journey 29

Chapter Seven: Reiki Holograms 35

Chapter Eight: Reiki Portals 39

Chapter Nine: Reiki Cords 43

Chapter Ten: Deepening Into the Angelic Realm 48

Chapter Eleen: Creating a Reiki Temple of Divine Light . . 62

Chapter Twelve: The Reiki Sanctuary and The Reiki Sphere of Divine Grace 67

Chapter Thirteen: Reiki Spinal Zap! 70

Chapter Fourteen: Reiki Family Constellation Session . . 74

Chapter Fifteen: Reiki DNA Blueprint Upgrade 78

Chapter Sixteen: Creating Your Own Reiki Affirmations . . 81

Chapter Seventeen: Reiki Crystal Healing Grid 85

Chapter Eighteen: Advanced Psychic Reiki Sessions . . 89

Chapter Nineteen: Psychic Reiki and Psychic Readings . . 135

Chapter Twenty: Mikao Usui's Five Reiki Principles of Reiki and the Psychic Reiki Code of Ethics 141

Chapter Twenty-One: Teaching Psychic Reiki 148

Chapter Twenty-Two: Planetary and Personal Time-Released Healings 153

Acknowledgments

I offer my gratitude to all those who have led me to write this book, as well as to all who have taught me along this sacred healing path. I give thanks to the Divine avatars Neem Karoli Baba, Amma, Mother Mary, and Jesus, for all their guidance and assistance. I give thanks to all the beings of light, the Deva of Reiki, archangel Raphael, my MAP team, and all the other invisible beings that assisted me in this process. I give thanks to my human teachers, both dead and living, including Mikao Usui, Jack Grey, Carolion, Michele Denis, Hethyrre, Alexandra Marquardt, and all my Reiki ancestors who were part of the lineage between Mikao Usui and myself. I give thanks to Omega Institute for maintaining a supportive environment for me to work in and share this gift of Reiki with their staff, R&R guests, and workshop participants. I give thanks to my wife Helema and my son Dylan for their love that is the guiding force in my life. And, I give thanks to you as the reader, for being willing to go on this journey with me into a special place of healing that if followed with commitment is bound to transform your life for the better.

Introduction

The book you hold in your hands is *conscious*. Yes, that is a very bold statement, yet one which is true. It is conscious in the sense that it can relate to you on the psychic level as you request it to send you healings, as well as be a guide for you to enter into deep meditative states. I know of no other book that is capable of this. If you want to sleep with this book under your pillow and ask it to send you Reiki, it will do so. If you are a bookstore owner and want this book to fill your store with healing Reiki light, it will do so upon your request. These simple techniques are shown in the chapters that follow, as are the explanations of how this book can perform these amazing acts.

We live in a time of miracles. My role as a teacher of Reiki is to point to the impossible and show my students how to do what some believe cannot be done. If you are someone entirely new to Reiki, this book can offer you a powerful and easy doorway into the world of Reiki healing. If you are someone already trained in Reiki, even up through the master level, this book can offer you ways of expanding your Reiki practice—advanced tools that even many Reiki masters may not have explored.

I honor the tradition of Reiki, and yet acknowledge that the tradition itself, as wonderful as it may be, is not the greatest teacher above all. The greatest teacher of Reiki is the Divine wisdom and consciousness of the energy itself. This book is empowered with that energy and consciousness. The invitation of this work is to open to that Divine consciousness and allow it to change your life for the better.

CHAPTER ONE

What is Psychic Reiki?

Psychic Reiki is the culminating work of my three previous books about Reiki, plus some new techniques, combined into one elegant and user-friendly energy healing system. As with traditional Reiki, this system acknowledges Mikao Usui as the founder of Reiki, and its practitioners access the Divine Life-Force energy known as Reiki for wellbeing and spiritual development. Yet this system differs from traditional Reiki in that there are no symbols or hand positions, since the practitioner learns to communicate with and direct the energy of Reiki telepathically.

Reiki is the world's most popular form of energy healing. Originally discovered by Mikao Usui, a Japanese mystic who lived from 1865 to 1926, Reiki is now flourishing around the world as a method of self care and wellbeing. It is even getting some recognition in Western medical circles, and is used as a form of palliative care in more progressive hospitals. Often, Reiki is translated from Japanese into English as meaning "Universal Life-Force Energy," and yet the Japanese kanji can also be translated to mean "Divine Life-Force Energy." I prefer the later translation, as it reflects the idea that Reiki does not really come from any person, or human, or even the collective field of life-force energy, but from a higher source that exists on the spiritual planes. As human channels for this energy, we can interpret it and create structures for understanding it, yet the energy itself is from the Divine, and thus not limited by our human structures or human interpretation. Reiki, as Divine Life-Force Energy, is an expression of Divine consciousness, and therefore always works for the highest good.

Reiki is most commonly taught as either a three- or four-degree system. Those teachers who teach it as a four-degree system essentially break the traditional third degree into two parts, but the essential teachings are the same whether one learns it as a three- or four-degree system.

First-degree Reiki empowers a student with an initiation from a Reiki master that is commonly called an attunement. This attunement involves the Reiki master putting sacred Reiki symbols into the student's crown chakra at the top of the head, as well as into the student's hands. Once activated to the energy of Reiki through the attunement, the student is then taught hand positions for doing a Reiki session on themself as well as Reiki hand positions for doing a session on another person. At this level, the student is usually not taught any of the Reiki symbols.

Second-degree Reiki training involves the student receiving another attunement from a Reiki master, and then learning three of the sacred Reiki symbols. One symbol makes the energy flow stronger. Another symbol focuses the energy for mental and emotional wellness. A third symbol is learned that allows a Reiki healer to send Reiki through time and space.

The third degree of Reiki, as I learned it, is the Master level, and it involves yet another attunement from a Reiki master, who then teaches three more Reiki symbols to the student. The student then learns how to initiate others to Reiki using these sacred Reiki symbols. Since some of these symbols also increase the ability of the Reiki student as a practitioner, some teachers separate the third degree into two parts. The first part serves to enhance ones skills as a practitioner and the second part is teacher training. Yet, as mentioned earlier, the teachings are essentially the same whether one learns Reiki as a three- or four-degree system. I have dear friends who are Reiki masters who learned it as a four-degree system and we respect each other's different styles, knowing the core teaching is still the same.

Reiki is a form of Divine light, and as a form of Divine light it is not limited by our human structures for accessing and interpreting it. I teach traditional Reiki workshops at one of the world's premier holistic retreat centers, Omega Institute, and have a great reverence for the Reiki symbols, the lineage, and the integrity of a system that has evolved now for almost a century to become the most popular form of energy healing in the world. Yet I am also open to there being more than what I know about Reiki and more than what I was taught by those who initiated me into Reiki. I know that these symbols and structures, as beautiful as they are, are simply human ways of accessing something far greater than our ability to totally comprehend. In 2007, I had a profound mystical experience while traveling in Laos that involved a visitation from the spirit of Mikao Usui, the person all Reiki lineages credit as the one who discovered Reiki. During that mystical experience I was given a ball of white light from Mikao Usui that went directly into my heart chakra. At the time, I simply thought that ball of white light contained information about Reiki, and during the weeks after that experience I became aware of information that became the bulk of my book *Reiki for Spiritual Healing* (Crossing Press, 2009). Eventually, after several years, I came to the awareness that that ball of white light included a new tool in the evolution of Reiki that I call "Mikao Usui's Reiki Crystal of Awakening."

Mikao Usui's Reiki Crystal of Awakening, which was first introduced to the general public through my book *New Reiki Software for Divine Living* (Ayni Books, 2013), is an energetic crystal made out of the light of Reiki. It holds Divine consciousness, information about Reiki, the ability to flow any energy from any Reiki symbol or any Reiki lineage, and can be psychically activated simply with a person's thoughts, though one can also use their voice. After writing *New Reiki Software for Divine Living*, I thought I had written everything about Reiki that I was supposed to write. I thought I had nothing new left to say on the subject of Reiki. Yet in the past six months I have been getting more information from my guides that there is more about Mikao Usui's Reiki Crystal of Awakening than I fully understood. Also, I have been shown that when combined with techniques from my first two Reiki books, an elegant healing system that is easy to access and also quite powerful is offered. The work of the following chapters offers these new Reiki possibilities as a unique Reiki system that I call Psychic Reiki.

Psychic Reiki has one primary tool — Mikao Usui's Reiki Crystal of Awakening — which, for the sake of brevity, I will refer to as the Reiki crystal from this point forward. Since this Reiki crystal can be activated simply though telepathic communication with it, the term *psychic* seems best suited to describe this new system of Reiki. This system of Reiki has no hand positions, no use of the traditional Reiki symbols, and no hierarchy of degrees that exists in traditional Reiki, such that anyone empowered to it can also initiate others to Psychic Reiki. Yet the energy Psychic Reiki draws from is still the same vibration of Reiki as traditional Reiki. Psychic Reiki simply accesses Reiki Divine Life-Force Energy in a way that fits more with the egalitarian evolution into an Aquarian Age. In other words, it is a new structure, a new human container for Reiki, though the energy of Reiki itself remains as pure and as Divine as it has always been.

Some of the most common techniques you will learn through the work of Psychic Reiki are listed below. If you recognize any from my previous books, know that they will be accessed at even deeper levels in this work as you grow deeper into your connection with your own Reiki crystal and that Divine presence which exists inside of that Reiki crystal.

Reiki, as a flow of energy used in traditional Reiki methods, will be able to flow now directly from your Reiki crystal. You will be able to access that flow of Reiki energy now psychically through your thoughts, or voice, to the specified area or target — usually to a person, place, or situation.

Reiki cords are an intense, continuous presence of Reiki between any two points in time/space. I often think of Reiki cords as miniature Reiki laser beams, and they can be more intense than many other Reiki tools. They can be created via a psychic request to your Reiki crystal, much easier than the Reiki cord techniques described in my first two Reiki books, *The Reiki Magic Guide To Self Attunement* and *Reiki for Spiritual Healing.*

Reiki meditations can be invoked when you ask your Reiki crystal to bring your consciousness, or the consciousness of an aspect of your being, such as an organ, cells, or even your subconscious mind, into the Reiki crystal, where it then marinates under the deep influence of that Divine consciousness that guides Reiki. Reiki meditations can have a requested specific focus or intent, such as inner peace, stress reduction, knowing Divine love, or any shift in consciousness that would be for the highest good.

Reiki holograms are objects made out of the Divine light that is Reiki. They can be anything, real or imagined. As a student of magic and spiritual esoteric studies I learned many years ago that thoughts themselves are considered real in magical theory. So, in a magical sense, even things that are imagined are real and can energetically influence us. Reiki holograms can often be useful as Reiki replications of specific organs and body parts, which, when fused into the physical organ, transfer an energetic Reiki imprint of that organ operating for the highest good. In truth, the only limit to creating Reiki holograms is your own imagination, and they can be of anything at all as long as they are for the highest good. Common Reiki holograms I use include Reiki holograms of angels, mythological power objects, natural objects, real-life archeological power sites such as the Great Pyramids, and the list goes on and on.

Reiki portals access the Reiki symbol called Hon Sha Ze Sho Nen Reiki used for sending Reiki through time and space, placing it strategically for heightened effect to cause a flow of energy (Reiki or otherwise) from one part of this magical universe into another part of this magical universe. A very common Reiki portal I use is to create one to the angelic realm, or directly to the archangel

Raphael, during a Reiki session, in the close proximity of the person being treated. This calls forth a direct flow of that angelic energy into the session as an additional force to accelerate the healing.

Reiki crystal grid is an entirely new and very potent technique. It does, however, require the presence of more than one Reiki crystal. To access this grid you can use your own Reiki crystal once you are empowered, as well as the Reiki crystal in this book. Or, if there are other Reiki healers present who are empowered to the Reiki crystal, you can invite all their Reiki crystals to also form a Reiki crystal grid. This technique works by uniting the power of more than one Reiki crystal to work in harmony with each other as one powerful grid of Reiki energy. The more Reiki crystals one can access for this technique, the more powerful the energy of that grid will be.

Reiki Sphere of Divine Grace is a huge bubble filled with Reiki light surrounding a person. It can be invoked upon request through your Reiki crystal. It has a very nurturing feeling, as if being held by the Mother of the Universe.

Reiki affirmations are affirmation phrases that have been empowered and infused with their own Reiki crystal, which is then programmed to send Reiki to a person as they speak the affirmation. A unique aspect of this work is that the Reiki being sent through each Reiki affirmation is specifically designed to work in perfect harmony with the intent of that affirmation. In other words, the energy of one Reiki affirmation will feel entirely unique and different than the Reiki of any other Reiki affirmation. In my book *New Reiki Software for Divine Living* I shared twenty-two of my own Reiki affirmations for anyone to use. Later in this book, you will be shown how to design and empower your very own Reiki affirmations, making them specific and tailor-made for you, as well as family and loved ones.

Reiki Constellation Therapy session is an energetic healing that works on the unconscious forces, bonds, and dynamics that exist within a family system. Although it does not send a direct session to any individual, it can address the energetic order or disorder that is the root cause of many individual issues within a specific family or group system.

Reiki DNA Blueprint Upgrade is exactly what is says, a spiritual upgrade of your own genetic being.

Most of the above techniques will be explored, each with its own chapter, later in this book.

CHAPTER TWO

The Psychic Reiki Initiation

This book that you are now reading is initiated with its own Reiki crystal. To demonstrate this, it will begin sending Reiki directly into your eyes now as you read this paragraph. You might feel Reiki flowing from the text of this paragraph into your eyes now. It could be that you are someone who is less energy sensitive, so to deepen the effect this book is now bringing your consciousness into the Reiki crystal of this book for a Reiki meditation for stillness and inner peace for the duration of time that you read this paragraph. Notice now if your consciousness seems to shift as you read this paragraph. Yes, you could say it is placebo effect from the suggestion that the book is sending you Reiki and that you are feeling more relaxed, yet, I trust that if you do the work of this book, your life will radically change for the better. That is not something I have ever known to happen simply through the placebo effect. So, keep on reading and doing the work that lies ahead, and you will step into a spiritual healing journey with the Divine.

If you want to become initiated into Psychic Reiki, know two things: First, just as with traditional Reiki, an initiation will change your overall energy vibration to a higher level. So, once you receive the initiation later in this chapter, know that you may go through some major changes in your life simply because your energy vibration will be at a higher level, and you will draw to you things which match that new higher vibration. Old things that were part of your life that contradict this new vibration may begin to fall away. For some, that may mean they change jobs or relationships, eat healthier, treat themselves with more kindness, or all the above. For others, it may mean a less dramatic shift on the outside but a deeper sense of wellbeing on the inside. Yet, know that once the initiation happens your life will change. That change will be for the better, but sometimes it may also be difficult in the short term as you adjust to it. The other thing you should know is that traditionally with Reiki there is supposed to be an energy exchange. Usually that means an exchange of money from the student to the Reiki master. It is said that students who do not complete the energy exchange never quite fully own their new Reiki ability, and this is something I experienced firsthand when I was a new Reiki master in 1995 and attuned several people for free. Even though Reiki would flow through their hands, it never seemed they fully grasped the healing potential that was now part of their very being.

The way I have addressed the Reiki energy exchange in my other Reiki books where an attunement is offered is that I suggest or recommend that in lieu of a large sum of money the reader perform some act of good works in their community as the energy exchange, since the attunement really is coming from the Divine anyway. In my other books I have made suggestions of what would be fitting in terms of an appropriate energy exchange, and have found some of my suggestions sometimes actually delayed a student from moving ahead with the attunement. Please know that it is simply intended that you do something good for someone without asking for anything in return. If that seems daunting or challenging, you can complete the energy exchange by simply posting a blessing to your family, friends, or community online under the hashtag #PsychicReiki. In our virtual online world the kindness of strangers adds up and can amount to huge shifts in our collective consciousness, so my hope is that contributing to a mountain of blessings online can be the failsafe method for anyone who might feel the energy exchange as an obstacle.

Meditate on what you feel is the most appropriate energy exchange for you to receive this energy healing initiation. Trust whatever your own inner voice tells you. Once you know what that is, commit to it. Then, prepare to engage the initiation by simply touching the Japanese kanji symbol for Reiki at the end of this chapter, which will activate the empowerment from this book to create in your energy field your own Reiki crystal. You may want to make this event a ritual process to enhance the feeling of it being special. For some that may mean lighting a candle, taking a cleansing bath with sea salt, or picking an important day such as a religious holiday, full moon, or even your birthday as a time to receive your initiation to the Reiki crystal. Or, it could be that you are someone who sees each day, each moment, as filled with the sacredness of the Divine and that you may want to move ahead right now with the initiation. Pause for a moment to reflect on which path is right for you, and then follow it. Once the time is right, whether that is right now or at some point in the future, take this book with you, lie down in a place where you will be undisturbed for at least fifteen minutes, and simply touch the Japanese kanji symbol for Reiki below. Once you touch it, the Reiki crystal inside this book will send you a Reiki session that will last about ten minutes and create a Reiki crystal in your own energy field, in front of the center of your chest about an inch in front of your heart chakra. That Reiki crystal is your Reiki crystal, and will respond to your telepathic or verbal requests to send Reiki for the rest of your life.

Touch the Japanese kanji symbol for Reiki to receive the Reiki crystal empowerment. After you touch it, simply lie down and receive the Reiki healing, which includes an energy transmission that will create a Reiki crystal in your own energy field, just in front of your heart chakra in the center of your chest.

CHAPTER THREE

Opening Your Heart to the Divine

Reiki always works for the highest good, and now you have
a powerful Reiki energetic tool imbued with Divine consciousness near your spiritual heart center. Think of that
and how powerful a statement that is. You now have an
energetic presence of Divine consciousness near your spiritual heart that will always be there for the rest of your life.
I think of the Reiki crystal as an energetic embodiment of
Divine grace, and now not only is that grace available to
you, but it is also part of your own energy system. In other
words, you yourself are an embodiment of Divine presence.
How wonderful that is!

   You may not completely own that Divine presence.
You may be tempted to try to run away from it. Yet that

is now impossible, because it is part of you. You might still judge yourself, deny the truth of your own Divinity, and play all kinds of mind games with yourself, which is part of the comedy of being human. You might ignore each word written on these pages because the fear of your own Divine light terrifies you. Imagine, if the Divine is part of you, how unstoppable your dreams suddenly become. I know that kind of existential stage fright, that level of terror which can arise when it becomes entirely clear that our most powerful dreams are easily within our grasp, if we would only dare to open our hands and reach.

The work of this chapter is in simply getting to know the Divine you. That is something you can do by working with and deepening your connection to the Divine consciousness inside the Reiki crystal.

Let's begin by working with some of the Reiki techniques mentioned in chapter one. Know as well that this book has its own Reiki crystal, and much of the emphasis in this book involves you simply being present while the Reiki crystal inside of this book works on you, which allows you to fully feel the results of specific techniques while in a passive and receptive state. Other times, you will be using your own Reiki crystal. There will also be times when your Reiki crystal and the one inside of this book work together.

Most of the world's great spiritual traditions say that the universe began with sound, with the Divine voice speaking creation into existence. In the Hindu tradition it is said that all of creation arises from the sacred sound of Om. The

Judeo-Christian traditions claim that the universe began when God said: *Let there be light!* I believe in the Divine, yet do not ascribe to the teachings of one tradition alone. My own personal belief is that the initial sound of creation began with Divine laughter, that the joy, the sorrow, the riddles, and mystery of life are best captured in this idea of a never-ending laugh, that the natural curve of time and space is Buddha (or Jesus or myriad other names) smiling.

The Reiki crystal inside of this book is now creating a Reiki portal in this paragraph connecting you with that Divine laughter. Allow yourself to simply rest your eyes here. Stop reading, and allow yourself to be bathed in that Divine laughter. Let yourself be in this presence energetically and to sink deeply into it. Let it soak into your mind, into your bones, into each organ and cell of your body. Feel it flow into your thoughts and the space between each thought. Feel it roll over each muscle, into your throat, into your lungs. With the next breath you take, allow this Divine laughter to come into your nose and mouth. Let it flow through your ears and come in through your eyes in all that you see, including this page, your fingers, and any-thing you see in the background behind this book. Know you are not alone, that you have never been alone, never will be nor ever could be. This Divine laughter has been with you always, and is part of you always. Even if you didn't see it or know it, that Divine presence has been there. It is our own illusion and confusion that leads to feel-ing separate from the Divine. Now, allow yourself to feel the Divine laughter flow into that illusion and confusion. All is a cosmic riddle, a gentle, infinite smile rising like a Möbius strip of one pair of lips kissing itself. Know anytime you feel alone you can open this book and read this page, or simply sit in front of it as this book lies open to this paragraph. Know as well that all this is happening through the Reiki crystal that is inside of this book and the Divine consciousness that exists inside of it. Everything written in this paragraph, and all the energy moving forth, is also possible within your own Reiki crystal, which lives now near your own spiritual heart. Think of this. Imagine the possibilities. Then, let go and stop reading for now.

Do you want to connect deeper now to your own Reiki crystal and the Divine consciousness that exists inside of it? If so, ask your Reiki crystal to send Reiki to open your heart to the Divine consciousness inside of the Reiki crystal. Ask this now by saying with your mind or your voice the following:

> *I invite my Reiki crystal to send Reiki to open my heart to the Divine consciousness inside of Mikao Usui's Reiki Crystal of Awakening. I ask for this now for the next ten minutes.*

Be still and notice any thoughts, sensations, or emotions that rise up in you as this healing continues. Then, add more layers to the healing by saying with your mind or your voice the following:

I invite my Reiki crystal to bring me into a Reiki meditation to open my heart to the Divine consciousness inside of Mikao Usui's Reiki Crystal of Awakening. I ask for this now for the next ten minutes.

Continue to be still, noticing any thoughts, sensations, or emotions that rise up in you as this healing continues. Then, add more layers to the healing by saying with your mind or your voice the following:

I invite my Reiki crystal to create a Reiki hologram of my brain infused with the Divine consciousness inside of Mikao Usui's Reiki Crystal of Awakening, and to fuse that into my physical brain now for the next ten minutes.

Continue to be still, and notice all thoughts, sensations, or emotions that may rise up in you as this healing deepens. Then, add more layers to the healing by saying with your mind or your voice the following:

I invite my Reiki crystal to work with the Reiki crystal in this book to create a Reiki crystal grid, and to put inside of this grid all my illusions of being separate from the Divine. I ask for this now for the next ten minutes.

Breathe into the stillness. Notice without judgment all thoughts, sensations, or emotions that move through you as this healing deepens. Then, add more layers to the healing by saying with your mind or your voice the following:

> *I invite my Reiki crystal to manifest around me, and my illusions of being separate from the Divine, a Reiki sphere of Divine grace. I ask for this now for the next ten minutes.*

Now, begin repeating to yourself the following Reiki affirmation:

> *I am one with Divine love*
> *I am one with Divine love*
> *I am one with Divine love*

Continue repeating this affirmation for the next ten minutes. Then, when you have finished, do nothing. Let this chapter go. Close the book. Go outside or do something entirely unrelated to the work of this book and see if that sense of Divine presence remains in your awareness. Don't try to hold on to it, as, in truth, it actually never fades and never can fade because it is eternally part of you and always has been. All that arises is the illusion of it fading. Notice this as well. Be kind to yourself. Be kind to others. Love what is, even if it makes no sense right now. Know that everything you experienced in this chapter is something you can revisit whenever you need or wish. It goes with you. It exists inside the Reiki crystal through the Divine consciousness residing there.

CHAPTER FOUR

Psychic Reiki Self Session

You now have your own Reiki crystal, and hopefully are becoming more aware of the Divine presence existing within it. Some who are highly energy sensitive might even feel the Reiki crystal's presence in their energy field. This crystal has Divine consciousness and will respond to your telepathic thoughts or your verbal requests. I normally suggest that a new student to the Reiki crystal begin by making soft verbal requests of the Reiki crystal first before moving on to direct telepathic communication with it. It isn't that telepathic communication with the Reiki crystal won't work, but simply that initially most students seem to prefer speaking to it.

Try the below sequence to experience your first Psychic Reiki self-healing session. Remember that the crystal itself is made of Reiki and Divine Consciousness, and sits in front of the heart chakra once a person is empowered to it.

A typical Psychic Reiki self-session involves simply using your thoughts or your voice to talk with the Reiki crystal and tell it to send Reiki to various systems in the body.

1. Ask your Reiki crystal to send Reiki to your brain and nervous system. Then allow a minute or so before moving on to the next request.

2. Ask your Reiki crystal to send Reiki to your digestive system, including your stomach, intestines both large and small, colon, esophagus, and any other aspect of the digestive system, such as enzymes, probiotic microbes, etc. Then allow a minute or so before moving on to the next request.

3. Ask your Reiki crystal to send Reiki to your circulatory system, including your heart, veins, arteries, capillaries, and all the blood that flows through them. Then allow a minute or so before moving on to the next request.

4. Ask your Reiki crystal to send Reiki to the your respiratory system, including the lungs, sinuses, nasal passages, and all the airways of your body. Then allow a minute or so before moving on to the next request.

5. Ask your Reiki crystal to send Reiki to your muscular system, including all muscles, ligaments, and tendons. Then allow a minute or so before moving on to the next request.

6. Ask your Reiki crystal to send Reiki to the your skeletal system, including all your bones, joints, cartilage,

skull, and all the vertebrae in your spine. Then allow a minute or so before moving on to the next request.

7. Ask your Reiki crystal to send Reiki to all your major glands and all your major organs, just in case there is anything that was overlooked. Then allow a minute or so before moving on to the next request.

8. Ask your Reiki crystal to send Reiki to all your chakras, those seven energetic centers of the human body integral to yoga and the Vedic healing systems. Allow a minute before moving on to the next request.

9. Ask your Reiki crystal to send Reiki to all your meridians, those energy pathways written about in Chinese medicine and in acupuncture. Allow a minute before moving on to the next request.

10. Ask your Reiki crystal to send Reiki to your mental body, which is simply the energetic aspect of your aura where your mental conditioning and mental patterns are held. Again, allow some time before moving on to the next request.

11. Ask your Reiki crystal to send Reiki to your emotional body, which is simply the energetic aspect of your aura where your emotional conditioning and patterns are held. Again, allow some time before moving on to the next request.

12. Ask your Reiki crystal to send Reiki to your karmic body, which is simply the energetic aspect of your being where your karmic conditioning and patterns are held. Again, allow some time before moving on to the next request.

13. Ask your Reiki crystal to create a Reiki Sphere of Divine Grace around you, which is like a huge bubble or egg filled with Reiki light completely surrounding you. Your Reiki crystal knows this, so all you have to do is ask it to create around you a Reiki Sphere of Divine Grace.

14. Ask your Reiki crystal to send a Reiki wave, which is a soothing ripple of Reiki from head to toe.

15. Ask your Reiki crystal to shift all lights to the most perfect and gentle form of integration.

Rest up after the session, and drink plenty of water, which helps your kidneys to process out any toxins that were released from your physical body during the session. Know you can repeat this session anytime you need it, and are encouraged to use it even when you may not feel like you need it, as it is by practicing this work that your entire life eventually will be bathed in this form of Divine light called Reiki.

CHAPTER FIVE

Psychic Reiki Session for Another Person

The basic session for working on another person is almost exactly the same as working on yourself. The sequence of requests you will make to your Reiki crystal is for the most part the same. However, there are a few things to note: First, unlike a traditional Reiki session, there are no hand positions involved. If the session is done in person, you can simply sit near the person you are working on. The person who is receiving the session should be wearing loose, comfortable clothing and lying down in a safe, neutral space, preferably a massage table. I strongly advise not giving a session to another person in person while they are in their own bed, or in your bed, as either case can send inappropriate subconscious messages. So, make sure the person receiving the session is in a safe and neutral space. If sending a session distantly, however, this is less of an issue since you are not present in the same room together and it does not have the same kind of implications.

Try the below sequence to experience your first Psychic Reiki healing session for another person. Remember that the crystal itself is made of Reiki and Divine Consciousness, and will send energy wherever you tell it to, no matter how near or far away the person receiving the session may be.

Make sure you use the person's name when making these requests. For example, if the person were named Joe, you would begin with: *I ask my Reiki crystal to send Reiki to Joe's brain and nervous system.* Talk to your Reiki crystal either using your thoughts or your voice, giving it the following commands:

1. Ask your Reiki crystal to send Reiki to the person's brain and nervous system. Then allow a minute or so before moving on to the next request.

2. Ask your Reiki crystal to send Reiki to the person's digestive system, including their stomach, intestines both large and small, colon, esophagus, and any other aspect of the digestive system, such as enzymes, probiotic microbes, etc. Then allow a minute or so before moving on to the next request.

3. Ask your Reiki crystal to send Reiki to their circulatory system, including heart, veins, arteries, capillaries, and all the blood that flows through them. Then allow a minute or so before moving on to the next request.

4. Ask your Reiki crystal to send Reiki to their respiratory system, including lungs sinuses, nasal passages, and all the airways of the body. Then allow a minute or so before moving on to the next request.

5. Ask your Reiki crystal to send Reiki to the person's muscular system, including all their muscles, ligaments, and tendons. Then allow a minute or so before moving on to the next request.

6. Ask your Reiki crystal to send Reiki to their skeletal system, including all the bones, joints, cartilage, skull, and vertebrae in their spine. Then allow a minute or so before moving on to the next request.

7. Ask your Reiki crystal to send Reiki to all their major glands and all their major organs, just in case there is anything that was overlooked. Then allow a minute or so before moving on to the next request.

8. Ask your Reiki crystal to send Reiki to all their chakras. Allow a minute before moving on to the next request.

9. Ask your Reiki crystal to send Reiki to all their meridians. Allow a minute before moving on to the next request.

10. Ask your Reiki crystal to send Reiki to the person's mental body. Again, allow some time before moving on to the next request.

11. Ask your Reiki crystal to send Reiki to their emotional body. Again, allow some time before moving on to the next request.

12. Ask your Reiki crystal to send Reiki to their karmic body. Again, allow some time before moving on to the next request.

13. Ask your Reiki crystal to create a Reiki Sphere of Divine Grace around the person, which is like a huge bubble or egg filled with Reiki light completely surrounding them. Your Reiki crystal knows this, so all you have to do is ask it to create around the person a Reiki Sphere of Divine Grace.

14. Ask your Reiki crystal to send a Reiki wave to the person, which is a soothing ripple of Reiki from head to toe. Repeat this several times.

15. Ask your Reiki crystal to shift all lights to the most perfect and gentle form of integration.

When it is appropriate, inform the person that they should drink plenty of water, and rest after the session. Drinking water is important since the Divine light of Reiki can knock loose old toxins held in the cells of a person's body. Though it is in the highest good to release those toxins at the cellular level, the process can be even more accelerated if they are well hydrated.

CHAPTER SIX

Reiki Meditation Journey

Reiki meditations are one of the most powerful yet underused aspects of the Reiki crystal. Remember, the Reiki crystal is imbued with Divine consciousness, so it can elicit many powerful states of awareness for those who learn to work with it effectively. What happens during a Reiki meditation is that, upon you requesting a Reiki meditation from your Reiki crystal, the Divine consciousness within that Reiki crystal draws your consciousness into the Reiki crystal, where it then marinates with Divine consciousness to shift your mental awareness. In my book *New Reiki Software for Divine Living* I wrote about Reiki meditations but did not fully understand how powerful and useful they can be. What follows in this chapter is a

Reiki meditation journey. You can think of it like a practice journey for you to fully grasp some of the energetic possibilities that can happen with a Reiki meditation from the Reiki crystal.

The Reiki crystal inside of this book will shortly be pulling you into a Reiki meditation. By continuing to read this text you are consenting to a Reiki meditation journey that will affect your consciousness and perhaps create altered states of consciousness. As you continue reading, the Reiki crystal inside of this book is now bringing you into a Reiki meditation for stillness and inner peace. Allow your consciousness to rest on the image below for as long as you wish to be in this meditation:

Draw your eyes away from the image when you want the Reiki meditation to end, and continue reading this text. Now, allow the Reiki crystal inside of this book to bring each cell of your body into a Reiki meditation for vibrancy, resilience, and supreme health. As you continue reading this text the Reiki crystal inside of this book is bringing the consciousness in each cell of your body into a deep Reiki meditation for vibrancy, joyful resilience, and supreme health. Allow your consciousness to rest on the image on the following page for as long as you wish to be in this meditation:

Know that as you draw your eyes away from the image, the Reiki meditation is released. But each time you re-focus on the image, the Reiki meditation returns. This is not happening because the book is sending you Reiki, but because it is activating the consciousness in each cell of your body to be in a Reiki meditation for vibrancy, joyful resilience, and supreme health.

Let's try a few more Reiki meditations just to explore the possibilities. Keep on reading and the next Reiki meditation from the Reiki crystal inside of this book is to feel Divine emptiness, that place of the void before anything came into the world of form. As you read this text the Reiki crystal inside of this book is bringing your consciousness into a Reiki meditation on Divine emptiness. Allow your thoughts to simply pass and know this meditation continues as you continue to read the text of this paragraph. Allow your consciousness to rest on the image below for as long as you wish to be in this meditation:

Know that as you draw your eyes away from the image, the Reiki meditation is released. But each time you re-focus on the image, the Reiki meditation returns. Another Reiki meditation that I would like to share is a Reiki flower meditation. Keep reading this text and the Reiki crystal inside of this book will bring your consciousness into a Reiki pink rose meditation, which elicits the sense of being surrounded by pink roses and being filled with their calming and heart-opening energy. Allow your eyes to rest on the image below for this Reiki pink rose meditation from the Reiki crystal inside this book to continue:

Draw your eyes away from the image; the Reiki meditation is released. Yet know each time you re-focus on the image, the Reiki meditation returns.

Reiki meditations can be quite creative. In my book *New Reiki Software for Divine Living* I shared forty-four Reiki meditation options, but I think the best Reiki meditations are the ones you discover yourself. You can ask your Reiki crystal to bring you into a Reiki meditation on just about anything, including relationships, work, life situations, and more. Below is the Reiki meditation template you can use to bring yourself into a Reiki meditation. Simply say the following words aloud or telepathically to your Reiki crystal:

I invite my Reiki crystal to bring me into a Reiki meditation for (describe the goal or state of consciousness).

You can also use your Reiki crystal to bring someone else into a Reiki meditation. It can be quite a wonderful tool either as a solo option for the person, or as a layered technique that is part of an advanced Reiki session. Know these meditations, like all forms of Reiki, only work for the highest good and cannot be used to coerce or manipulate others. They can only be used to heal and assist someone on their spiritual journey. Simply say the following words aloud or telepathically to your Reiki crystal:

I invite my Reiki crystal to bring (name of person into a Reiki meditation for (describe the goal or state of consciousness).

What happens when you ask your Reiki crystal to perform a Reiki meditation on another person or group of people is that it draws the recipient's consciousness into your Reiki crystal. In a one-on-one healing that isn't so noticeable for you as the healer, but when doing large-scale group healings of twenty or more people it can be quite amazing to feel everyone's consciousness suddenly be drawn into your Reiki crystal. And, remember, you can also ask your Reiki crystal to bring the consciousness of the cells of your body (or another person's body) into

Reiki meditations as well. Reiki meditations can be a very profound healing technique to use for healing organs and organ systems where the disease is heavily engrained in the cellular consciousness of the person, shifting a person's consciousness into a more serene state, or even shape-shifting their awareness to explore new possibilities.

CHAPTER SEVEN

Reiki Holograms

The concept of Reiki holograms is explored in my book *Reiki for Spiritual Healing* (Crossing Press, 2009), but I include this chapter here because Reiki holograms can now be created much easier than before by using your Reiki crystal. Also, integrating Reiki holograms into the healing process can be very powerful, while also opening avenues for you as a healer into Divine imagination, which for me is the end goal of all healing.

A Reiki hologram is an energetic device made out of the light that is Reiki. Often in traditional Reiki the energy of Reiki is experienced more as a constant flow or wave of energy. But, with Reiki holograms, it is as if that light of Reiki is becoming condensed, the same way light in our universe becomes condensed to form matter, as noted in Einstein's formula $E=MC^2$. In this more condensed state, Reiki can exist as a particular form, rather than a flow or wave of energy. You can create Reiki holograms of virtually anything, *even things that exist only in the realm of imagination.* What a Reiki hologram does depends to some degree on what you are creating as a Reiki hologram. For example, I often create Reiki holograms of organs during a healing and then infuse that Reiki hologram into the actual organ. What this does is effectively raise the energetic vibration of the real organ to a higher healing vibration. I also sometimes have used Reiki holograms of a person's brain and nervous system in a deep Theta wave, then infused that Reiki hologram into the person's brain and nervous system to help them relax or fall asleep. You can also create Reiki holograms of sacred sites, and in those cases the Reiki hologram will elicit an energy vibration of that sacred site. Experience this now in the next few paragraphs as the book will create a Reiki hologram around you of several such sacred sites. Allow your eyes to rest for a period of time on each paragraph, as the Reiki holograms will be released once your eyes look away.

The Reiki crystal inside this book is now creating around you a Reiki hologram of the sarcophagus in the Kings Chamber of the Great Pyramid of Giza in Egypt. The impact of this Reiki hologram is to be maintained for as long as you gaze at this paragraph. Once your eyes move to the next paragraph, the Reiki hologram will be released.

The Reiki crystal inside this book is now creating around you a Reiki hologram of Bayon Temple in Angkor Wat, the great Buddhist temple in Cambodia. The impact of this Reiki hologram is to be maintained for as long as you gaze at this paragraph. Once your eyes move to the next paragraph, the Reiki hologram will be released.

The Reiki crystal inside of this book is now creating around you a Reiki hologram of Stonehenge. The impact of this Reiki hologram is to be maintained for as long as you gaze at this paragraph. Once your eyes move to the next paragraph, the Reiki hologram will be released.

One of my favorite uses of Reiki holograms involves creating Reiki holograms of my own hands performing a Kabbalistic laying on of hands technique called Healing Emanation, a very simple but profound technique that simply involves laying your hands on someone and intending that infinite Divine presence with them come into you. Since that presence is infinite, it doesn't drain the other person, and instead actually causes a healing in them as that Divine presence rises up through them to come into you. When I do this as a Reiki hologram session, it has an effect similar to me performing the healing with my own hands. I tend to use this technique quite often when doing group sessions where it would be impossible to place my hands on everyone in the room, and also during distant sessions. Try this now by using the following template to experience Reiki holograms of your own hands performing Healing Emanation on yourself. Say the following either out loud or telepathically to your Reiki crystal:

> *I ask my Reiki crystal to create a Reiki hologram of my hands, and to place these Reiki holograms on my belly, performing Healing Emanation on me for the next ten minutes.*

Then sit back, relax, and enjoy the session.

CHAPTER EIGHT

Reiki Portals

There is a symbol in Reiki called Hon Sha Ze Sho Nen that is used for distant healing. In my experiments with advanced Reiki crystal techniques, I learned that you can ask your Reiki crystal to place that Reiki symbol as a Reiki portal between any two points in time and space, and, that if you intend, energy can then flow between these two points. That energy does not even have to be Reiki, though if it were used for some purpose other than the highest good the technique would not work, since Reiki, your Reiki crystal, and all Reiki symbols can only work for the highest good. I use Reiki portals normally to connect with higher-level beings and bring their energy into a session. However, one can also use Reiki portals to connect with powerful healing energies elsewhere on the planet, or even in other parts of the universe.

One interesting use of Reiki portals is to put them in a room, connecting the energy of that room with an avatar such as Jesus or Amma, and notice the energetic shift that happens. Try this now using the template below, and communicating with your Reiki crystal either verbally or telepathically:

> *I ask my Reiki crystal to create a Reiki portal to (name Jesus, Amma, Krishna, or some other incarnation of the Divine) and to place that Reiki portal in the center of this room for the next ten minutes.*

Notice the energy in the room before and after the portal is created. Allow yourself to be one with this energy for as long as you need. And know you can access it anywhere, anytime by simply using your Reiki crystal to create a Reiki portal.

I will often use a similar template to create a Reiki portal to cosmic string. Cosmic strings, in theoretic terms, are like fault lines that bind the universe together. Yet, in more esoteric studies like remote viewing, many students have found that when remote viewing cosmic string it feels like an energetic rebalancing. Thus, I often create Reiki portals to cosmic string to bring an energetic rebalancing into a space.

> *I ask my Reiki crystal to create a Reiki portal to cosmic string, and to place that Reiki portal in the center of this room for the next ten minutes.*

Notice the energy in the room before and after the portal is created. Allow yourself to enjoy this energy for as long as you need.

The most exciting and new healing technique I have explored with Reiki portals is placing them inside the human body. I only do this when connecting with Divine beings, such as avatars and angels. Often, I will ask my Reiki crystal to create a Reiki portal to Jesus, inside of a diseased organ, so His healing light can be brought directly into that organ. Below is the template for this:

> *I ask my Reiki crystal to create a Reiki portal to Jesus, and to place that Reiki portal in (name the diseased organ or area of the body) for the next ten minutes.*

Reiki portals can also be closed quickly if you find the energy that they have connected you to is at all overwhelming or making you feel ungrounded. To close a Reiki portal, simply ask your Reiki crystal to close it, asking with either your thoughts or your voice. An example follows, again communicating directly with your Reiki crystal either through your thoughts or your voice:

> *I ask my Reiki crystal to close the Reiki portal it just created.*

Reiki portals are powerful tools to use. Remember, you can always close them if the energy feels overwhelming to you or anyone involved with the session. In the following chapter, you will be shown how to combine working with Reiki portals and Reiki holograms to connect deeper to the angelic realm.

CHAPTER NINE

Reiki Cords

Reiki cords are like mini Reiki laser beams that can be placed by your Reiki crystal between any two points in time or space. They are explored in my book The *Reiki Magic Guide to Self Attunement* (Crossing Press, 2007) as an energetic tool that one can access through working with your Higher Self. However, with the recent advancements in the evolution of Reiki, they are now much easier to use by accessing them through your Reiki crystal. I love working with Reiki cords, as they can intensify a session by either sending cords through time or through various geometric angles into a specific area being treated. For example, whenever I feel myself coming down with a chest cold I will use my Reiki crystal to create Reiki cords from the left side of my rib cage to the right side of my rib cage, so that there are these laser-like beams of Reiki light flowing between these points through both of my lungs. Also, I will ask my Reiki crystal to create Reiki cords through each of my lungs along a specific time line, usually from present time back until a few hours before the chest cold began. The opportunities to use Reiki cords are relatively endless, and limited only by your imagination and the requirement that you respect the free will of others. I will not create Reiki cords that may impact someone else without their consent.

Think first before asking your Reiki crystal to create a Reiki cord or set of cords. You will want to imagine how best to angle a cord through the area where the healing is needed. For example, when working on my lungs it makes perfect sense to link the Reiki cords from one side of my rib cage to the next side. If I were working on my throat, which I sometimes do when feeling a sore throat coming on, I would anchor one Reiki cord from the left side of my jaw bone to the right side of my collar bone, and then another from the right side of my jaw bone to the left side of my collar bone, making an X of Reiki cords in my throat. Again, depending on the area that needs the Reiki session you should think of where the best place is to anchor the Reiki cords. Once you have decided where to place them, simply follow the template below to create the Reiki cords. Know they are manifested directly by the Reiki crystal, so the cumbersome language used in some of my previous books when working with the Higher Self is not necessary with this approach.

Some recommended Reiki cord templates that I use quite often follow in the next few paragraphs. Explore working with them, and see how you like the results. Know that you can create your own Reiki cord options as well. Do not feel limited by these few templates, as they are just stepping stones intended to take you forward on your own journey with this technique.

> *I ask my Reiki crystal to create a Reiki cord between my left hand and my right hand and to manifest this now for the next ten minutes.*

Now, once the Reiki cords between your hands are activated, try moving your hands and placing them on both sides of your torso to see if you can sense the intensity of the Reiki cords flowing between your hands. Then, move your hands so they are on each side of your head, and again notice the sensation of Reiki flowing. If you are not energy sensitive and cannot feel the energy, do not worry, simply hold them in place for a minute or so and see if you feel calmer or more at peace while the Reiki cords are flowing. Then, place your hands on either side of your leg, again paying attention to the energy flow whenever possible. Continue playing with the energy and different hand positions until the Reiki cords expire after the ten minutes is complete, knowing that it is through play that we often discover our true abilities.

Below is another Reiki cord option you can explore, related to clearing the spine. I first began using this technique when getting chiropractic adjustments on a regular basis in San Francisco. Although the session is not a full replacement for a real chiropractic adjustment, I did find that when using this on a regular basis I didn't need to see the chiropractor quite as often.

> *I ask my Reiki crystal to create a Reiki cord between each vertebra of my spine and to manifest this now for the next ten minutes.*

Allow this Reiki cord healing to unwind the tension and any stuck energy held in your spine. This is a nice one to use at night before you go to bed.

Using Reiki cords through time can also be very powerful. I often run Reiki cords through the karmic body when a person is in need of intensive healing, sometimes even running those Reiki cords through many lifetimes. Normally I keep this use of Reiki cords relatively short due to the level of intensity. Before ever using this technique on another person it is best to use it first on yourself so you fully understand the healing potential involved. Try this template at a time when you have enough time to fully process a deep healing. Even though the healing itself is relatively short, it is quite powerful:

I ask my Reiki crystal to create a Reiki cord through my karmic body, through time from the present moment backwards in time to the moment my soul first split off from the Divine, and to manifest this now for the next five minutes.

Now lie down or sit quietly and let the deep healing release whatever energetic debris is ready to be released at this point in time from all of your lifetimes. Know you can always repeat this session as often as you wish, so it is better to keep it short rather than experience a longer healing that potentially might be energetically overwhelming. If at any time the session does feel overwhelming, simply ask your Reiki crystal to end it immediately. When the session is complete, then ask your Reiki crystal to perform a short session on you for integration using the template below:

I ask my Reiki crystal to perform a Reiki integration session on me for as long as is for my highest good.

When the integration is complete, drink plenty of water. Reiki cords are powerful tools and now very easy to access through your Reiki crystal. Use them wisely.

CHAPTER TEN

Deepening Into the Angelic Realm

Reiki is a wonderful tool for self healing. In the previous chapters you were shown basic techniques for performing a self session as well as a session on another person, plus Reiki meditations, Reiki holograms, and Reiki portals. Once you have fully integrated that knowledge and made it a daily practice, you can then layer even more advanced Reiki crystal techniques into the session for a deeper level of healing. One powerful avenue for that is through using Reiki to work with the angelic realm.

Angels are pure spiritual beings created by the Divine. They operate at a higher vibration than most humans, but can occasionally be seen, felt, and communicated with. They are known for their tireless presence assisting and comforting those in need, offering insight and healing when it is requested. The most popular and well-known angels, at least in the Western world, are the archangels Michael, Gabriel, Uriel, and Raphael. But there are other archangels as well, such as the archangel Metatron, who is often referred to in certain Jewish mystical and related esoteric texts as the *Lesser Jaweh*, and is considered by some to be the highest angel of all. Even though Metatron is not as well known in popular culture as those angels previously named, that does not diminish the power and might of this angel. In the text that follows, you will be able to deepen your energetic connection to Metatron and many other angels though Reiki portals and Reiki meditations. All you will need to do is read the text, as the Reiki crystal inside of this book will create the healing.

I recommend you work through this chapter slowly, connecting to one angel at a time on a daily basis to form a relationship with each. As you continue this work, you may find some angels appeal to you more than others. That is totally fine and natural. In developing your relationship to them it is completely fine to have your favorites, the ones you will be drawn to the most. Usually part of that is also due to your own needs and how that matches or doesn't match with an angel's specific talents and abilities. For example, I often work with the archangel Raphael, who governs healing. That doesn't mean I never connect or work with other angels, but just that I work with Raphael more than others. I find the best way to learn about angels is through direct experience with them, something that the following paragraphs provide. One additional item to note is that it is my own belief that angels do not have a specific gender. Though most of the names of common angels are male, and they are often depicted in artwork as male, that is more a result of them being viewed through a strong patriarchal religious lens for the past few thousand years. The beings themselves, when I sense them energetically, are beyond the categories of gender.

Metatron is considered a guardian of the Tree of Life, a patron angel of children, and is known to help people discover their spiritual power. This book is now opening a Reiki portal between you and Metatron through the words of this paragraph. As you read this text, and as long as you look at it, even if not reading it directly, this Reiki portal will remain in effect. Tune in to this energetic presence of Metatron as the Reiki portal remains open between the two of you. Close your eyes for a moment, and simply allow yourself to experience this angelic presence. Sit quietly in this powerful energy. Now the Reiki crystal inside of this book is bringing your consciousness into a deep Reiki meditation on your relationship with Metatron. Be in silence with this meditation and allow it to go deeper as the Reiki crystal inside of this book brings you and Metatron together into a deep Reiki meditation. This means that your consciousness, as well as the consciousness of Metatron, and the Divine consciousness inside of the Reiki crystal in this book are all co-existing together, marinating and being mutually aware of each other. Allow this to happen, to sink your consciousness even deeper into this presence of the Divine and the archangel Metatron. Let yourself sit silently for several minutes in this presence. Then, if you wish, ask a question of Metatron either out loud or with your mind. Hear the response, which may come to you as a word, an image, even a sensation, or simply as an intuitive knowing. Know you can revisit this paragraph anytime you wish, anytime you want to experience or deepen that connection to Metatron. You can also use your own Reiki crystal at any time to create a Reiki portal to Metatron and/or lead you into a Reiki meditation with or about Metatron. All you need to do to activate this is make a request to your Reiki crystal either through your mind or your voice.

Michael is one of the most loved and well-known archangels, often known for the power of protection. Paintings and sculptures depicting this archangel usually show Michael holding a sword, referencing a sense of spiritual might. As a protector, this angel can assist in removing and releasing harmful energies or warding off any such energy. Feel the presence of Michael now as the Reiki crystal inside of this book is opening a Reiki portal inside of this text between you and the archangel Michael. Close your eyes for a moment and see if you can feel, sense, or even just imagine Michael's powerful sword protecting you and clearing you from anything that may cause you harm. Now, the Reiki crystal inside of this book is bringing you into a deep Reiki meditation on your relationship with Michael.

Be still and allow your consciousness to be drawn deeper and deeper into the Reiki crystal as this meditation unfolds. Listen and grow quiet as the Reiki crystal inside of this book now brings you and Michael together into a deep Reiki meditation. Your consciousness, as well as the consciousness of Michael, and the Divine consciousness of the Reiki crystal are all now co-existing together within the Reiki crystal inside of this book, being mutually aware of each other. Allow this to happen, to sink your consciousness even deeper into this presence of the Divine and the archangel Michael. Let yourself sit silently for several minutes in this presence. Ask any questions you may have for this powerful angel. Hear the response, which may come to you as a word, an image, even a sensation, or simply as an intuitive knowing. Know you can revisit this paragraph anytime you wish, anytime you want to experience or deepen that connection to Michael. Also, know that with your own Reiki crystal you can open a Reiki portal to Michael at any time, as well as connect even deeper to this angel by requesting your Reiki crystal bring you into a Reiki meditation with Michael. A favorite technique I often use is to open a Reiki portal to Michael over myself, my loved ones, even my car or home whenever I feel a need for any of these to be protected. Try this in your own life, and you will likely be amazed at the results.

Gabriel is a powerful angel who plays an important role in the religious texts of Judaism, Christianity, and Islam. The name Gabriel means "God is my strength," and this angel is commonly viewed as a Divine messenger. Christian texts refer to Gabriel as the angel who informed Mary that she would conceive and give birth to Jesus. Islamic texts credit Gabriel as the angel who appeared to the prophet Mohammed and dictated to him the entire Qur'an, the most holy book of Islam. In the Jewish Torah it is claimed that Gabriel offered insight and understanding to the prophet Daniel. Using Reiki techniques from this book to connect with the angel Gabriel is a wonderful way to gain insight about your own life. This book is now opening a Reiki portal between you and Gabriel through the words of this paragraph. As you read this text, and as long as you look at it, even if not reading it directly, this Reiki portal will remain in effect. Tune in to this energetic presence of Gabriel as the Reiki portal remains open between the two of you. Close your eyes for a moment, and simply allow yourself to experience this angelic presence. Sit quietly in the powerful energy of this Divine messenger. Now the Reiki crystal inside of this book is bringing your consciousness into a deep Reiki meditation on your relationship with Gabriel. Be in silence with this meditation, and now allow it to go deeper as the Reiki crystal inside of this book brings you and Gabriel together into a deep Reiki meditation. This means that your consciousness, as well as the consciousness of Gabriel, and the Divine consciousness inside of the Reiki crystal in this book are all co-existing together, marinating and being mutually aware of each other. Allow this to happen, to sink your consciousness even deeper into this presence of the Divine and the archangel Gabriel. Let yourself sit silently for several minutes in this presence. Then, if you wish, ask Gabriel to offer you a message from the Divine. Hear the response, which may come to you as a word, an image, even a sensation, or simply as an intuitive knowing. Know you can revisit this paragraph anytime you wish, anytime you want to experience or deepen that connection to Gabriel. You can also use your own Reiki crystal at any time to create a Reiki portal to Gabriel, and/or lead you into a Reiki meditation with or about Gabriel. All you need to do to activate this is make a request to your Reiki crystal either through your mind or your voice.

Uriel is not mentioned by name in the Bible but does appear in the *Book of Enoch* and other mystical Jewish texts, some related to the Kabbalah, as well as Gnostic Christian texts. Uriel's name means "Light of God," and this powerful angel is often known as the angel of peace. Feel the presence of Uriel now as the Reiki crystal inside of this book is opening a Reiki portal inside of this text between you and the archangel Uriel. Close your eyes for a moment, and see if you can feel, sense, or even just imagine Uriel's peaceful presence flowing out to you and bringing a deep sense of calm and quiet. Now the Reiki crystal inside of this book is bringing you into a deep Reiki meditation on your relationship with Uriel. Be still and allow your consciousness to be drawn deeper and deeper into the Reiki crystal as this meditation unfolds. Listen and grow quiet as the Reiki crystal inside of this book now brings you and Uriel together into a deep Reiki meditation. Your consciousness, as well as the consciousness of Uriel, and the Divine consciousness of the Reiki crystal are all now co-existing together within the Reiki crystal inside of this book, being mutually aware of each other. Allow this to happen, to sink your consciousness even deeper into this presence of the Divine and the archangel Uriel. Let yourself sit silently for several minutes in this presence. Ask any questions you may have of this powerful angel. Hear the response, which may come to you as a word, an image, even a sensation, or simply as an intuitive knowing. Know you can revisit this paragraph anytime you wish, anytime you want to experience or deepen that connection to Uriel.

Raphael is the archangel most known for healing, and this angel's name can be translated as "God Heals." As I mentioned before, this is the angel I work with the most. That does not mean you will, as you certainly may resonate more with the qualities of other angels. Also, know your connection to each angel may change over time as you grow and evolve. Yet, now, in this moment at least, I want to invite you to connect with this healing archangel. This book is now opening a Reiki portal between you and Raphael through the words of this paragraph. As you read this text, and as long as you look at it, even if not reading it directly, this Reiki portal will remain in effect. Tune in to this energetic presence of Raphael as the Reiki portal remains open between the two of you. Close your eyes for a moment, and simply allow yourself to experience this healing angelic presence. Sit quietly in the powerful energy of this Divine healer. Know the Reiki crystal inside of this book is bringing your consciousness into a deep Reiki meditation on your relationship with Raphael. Be in silence with this meditation, and now allow it to go deeper as the Reiki crystal inside of this book brings you and Raphael together into a deep Reiki meditation. This means that your consciousness, as well as the consciousness of Raphael, and the Divine consciousness inside of the Reiki crystal in this book are all co-existing together, marinating and being mutually aware of each other. Allow this to happen, to sink your consciousness even deeper into this presence of the Divine and the archangel Raphael. Let yourself sit silently for several minutes in this presence. Then, if you wish, ask Raphael to offer you a healing insight. Hear the response, which may come to you as a word, an image, even a sensation, or simply as an intuitive knowing. Know you can revisit this paragraph anytime you wish, anytime you want to experience or deepen that connection to Raphael. You can also use your own Reiki crystal at any time to create a Reiki portal to Raphael and/or lead you into a Reiki meditation with or about Raphael. All you need to do to activate this is make a request to your Reiki crystal either through your mind or your voice. One technique I often use, which you can do with your own Reiki crystal, is to ask that it create a Reiki portal to Raphael, placing the portal inside of your body, often near a wound or area of illness to accelerate the healing. This Reiki portal then begins to flow this archangel's powerful healing light directly into the area of the body where it is most needed. Try this on your own if you wish, as it can be a very powerful healing technique.

Sandalphon is an archangel often referred to as the twin of Metatron. Some writings also refer to Sandalphon as the human prophet Elijah elevated to angelic status. Sandalphon is known as the angel of music and prayer. Feel the presence of Sandalphon now as the Reiki crystal inside of this book is opening a Reiki portal inside of this text between you and the archangel Sandalphon. Close your eyes for a moment, and see if you can feel, sense, or even just imagine this archangel. Now the Reiki crystal inside of this book is bringing you into a deep Reiki meditation on your relationship with Sandalphon. Be still and allow your consciousness to be drawn deeper and deeper into the Reiki crystal as this meditation unfolds. Listen and grow quiet as the Reiki crystal inside of this book now brings you and Sandalphon together into a deep Reiki meditation. Your consciousness, as well as the consciousness of Sandalphon, and the Divine consciousness of the Reiki crystal are all now co-existing together within the Reiki crystal inside of this book, being mutually aware of each other. Allow this to happen, to sink your consciousness even deeper into this presence of the Divine and the archangel Sandalphon. Let yourself sit silently for several minutes in this presence. Send any prayers you may have to this powerful angel. Hear the response, which may come to you as a word, an image, even a sensation, or simply as an intuitive knowing.

Know you can revisit this paragraph anytime you wish, anytime you want to experience or deepen that connection to Sandalphon. Also, know that with your own Reiki crystal you can open a Reiki portal to Sandalphon at any time, as well as connect even deeper to this angel by requesting your Reiki crystal bring you into a Reiki meditation with Sandalphon.

Raziel is the archangel of Divine wisdom, mysteries, and esoteric secrets. I often invoke this angel when working on new discoveries related to energy healing, whether it is Reiki or other techniques. Know that this angel can be of great assistance in taking your spiritual and healing journey to the next level, far beyond what any book written by a human being can offer. This book is now opening a Reiki portal between you and Raziel through the words of this paragraph. As you read this text, and as long as you look at it, even if not reading it directly, this Reiki portal will remain in effect. Tune in to this energetic presence of Raziel as the Reiki portal remains open between the two of you. Close your eyes for a moment, and simply allow yourself to experience this wise angelic presence. Sit quietly in the powerful energy of this keeper of Divine secrets and wisdom. Now the Reiki crystal inside of this book is bringing your consciousness into a deep Reiki meditation on your relationship with Raziel. Be in silence with this meditation, and now allow it to go deeper as the Reiki crystal inside of this book brings you and Raziel together into a deep Reiki meditation. This means that your consciousness, as well as the consciousness of Raziel, and the Divine consciousness inside of the Reiki crystal in this book are all co-existing together, marinating and being mutually aware of each other. Allow this to happen, to sink your consciousness even deeper into this presence of the Divine and the archangel Raziel. Let yourself sit silently for several minutes in this presence. Then, if you wish, ask Raziel to offer you an insight of spiritual wisdom. Hear the response, which may come to you as a word, an image, even a sensation, or simply as an intuitive knowing. Know you can revisit this paragraph anytime you wish, anytime you want to experience or deepen that connection to Raziel.

The angels mentioned here are just a few of the many you can access and work with using these techniques. Any of the techniques shown in the paragraphs above can be adapted and used by your own Reiki crystal. As an author, I enjoy creating Reiki portals within a written text, but one could just as easily create the same Reiki portals in their own altar, room, candle, drawing, or anything else that would be appropriate as a gateway to these powerful Divine beings.

You can also make it a practice to open Reiki portals to the angelic realm without specifying which particular angel you want to connect with. I often use this technique when performing large group healings, since in those situations each person's need in the healing may be quite different that the need of others in the same room. Another secondary technique you can use related to angels is to invite your

Reiki crystal to create a Reiki hologram of an angel in a specific area or space. This simply magnifies an energetic Reiki signature and replicates a presence of that angel within the space named. It isn't that the Reiki hologram is an actual angel, but it will carry an energetic presence that will alter the space energetically in a manner similar to the presence of an actual angel. Try this the next time you perform a Reiki self session. Create Reiki holograms of one or more angels in the room. You can do this by simply using the template below:

> *I invite my Reiki crystal to create a Reiki hologram of the angel (name which one)*
> *and to place this Reiki hologram (say where you would like the Reiki hologram to be placed)*
> *for the next (say how many) minutes.*

You can always release a Reiki hologram of an angel before the original number of minutes. If you need to do this, simply do so by telling your Reiki crystal:

> *I invite my Reiki crystal to now release the Reiki hologram of the angel (name which one).*

Once you ask your Reiki crystal to release the Reiki hologram of the angel, that Reiki hologram then vanishes into emptiness. Know as well that the placement and positioning of the Reiki hologram of an angel can be important.

During healings I will often ask my Reiki crystal to create Reiki holograms of the archangel Raphael, placed so that holograms of the archangel are touching a person's shoulder to bring healing comfort. You might be surprised how often the person being worked on tells me afterward that they felt an angel touching them during the healing.

Since Reiki holograms of angels are simply energetic replications of real angels, you can actually create numerous Reiki holograms of the same angel simultaneously during the same healing. Again, this is something I often do when performing large group healings where I ask my Reiki crystal to create a Reiki hologram, usually of the archangel Raphael, next to each person in the room. The energetic shift that happens when I use this technique is quite strong and palpable to those sensitive to energy healing.

CHAPTER ELEVEN

Creating a Reiki Temple of Divine Light

My first book, *The Reiki Magic Guide To Self Attunement* (Crossing Press, 2007), advocated that Reiki is far more than just a healing modality, more than the paid-for Reiki sessions and trainings, which are certainly wonderful, yet which do not fully embody the scope of all that is possible with Reiki. That book claimed Reiki should be part of every aspect of our lives, and offered tools for anyone to be able to access Reiki energy. Since the publication of that book, Reiki has continued to evolve, and the evolution of Mikao Usui's Reiki Crystal of Awakening now makes that possibility outlined in my first book even easier to attain. I do not see Reiki itself as a religion, but I do feel and know its potential to deepen a person's connection to the Divine, regardless of what name one gives to the Divine. As that spiritual aspect of an individual grows and deepens, it can bring healing into every aspect of a person's life, changing how we relate to our friends, family, community, and ourselves. Creating moments of communion with highly evolved spiritual beings only deepens that Divine presence in our lives even more.

Creating a Reiki Temple of Divine Light will eventually be part of the process you can use when performing healings on others. Yet, for now, it is best to learn how to create one when you are doing a Reiki healing on yourself.

Begin by asking your Reiki crystal to create a Reiki portal in each wall of the room where you are doing the self session. Ask that these Reiki portals each be to highly-evolved spiritual beings, such as Buddha, Jesus, Mother Mary, Neem Karoli Baba, Mikao Usui, Kwan Yin, or even living avatars, such as Amma. The choice of which spiritual beings you want to create Reiki portals to should be made following your own guidance. Those above are just suggestions.

Once you have created Reiki portals in each wall, notice how it changes the energy in the room. You can then layer this effect even deeper by creating a Reiki portal in the ceiling to the angelic realm. If you have a massage table, you may want to add a Reiki portal inside of it to the archangel Raphael or some other spiritual being that is known for healing attributes so that their energy flows directly through the table.

Now, ask your Reiki crystal to create a Reiki portal in the floor to a particular power center on the planet, such as the sacred volcano of Mount Shasta, the healing waters of Lourdes, or even a specific temple or historic location known for its powerful healing energy. Some places I would recommend experimenting creating Reiki portals to are Angkor Wat, the sacred temple in Cambodia; Machu Picchu, the well-known sacred historic site in the Andes mountains of Peru; Stonehenge, the powerful prehistoric monument in England; and the Great Pyramids of Egypt, as well as the Sphinx. Once you have asked your Reiki crystal to create a Reiki portal in the floor to a particular power center on the earth, simply notice how the room now feels.

You should now have Reiki portals existing in each wall, plus the floor and ceiling, all connecting to someone, or something, that will add more Divine light into the space where you are performing the self session. Now, ask your Reiki crystal to create around the entire room a Reiki Sphere of Divine Grace, which, as mentioned in the first chapter of this book, is like a huge bubble or egg filled with Reiki light. This will add a layer of nurturing light to the space. Try this now and simply notice how the space feels to you.

Once you have created this outer layer of your temple, begin working on the inner aspects. Ask your Reiki crystal to create around you, or the person being healed, a Reiki hologram of the sarcophagus in the Kings Chamber in the

Great Pyramid of Egypt. Give a specific number of minutes that you would like this Reiki hologram to remain intact, which should be for all the estimated time of the healing. If, for example, you were doing a half hour long healing, you would likely want to create this Reiki hologram to last for thirty minutes. Try this now, asking your Reiki crystal to create around you a Reiki hologram of the sarcophagus in the Kings Chamber in the Great Pyramid of Egypt.

The power of this sacred site can be energetically replicated by the Reiki hologram. Although it is not exactly as powerful as it would be experiencing the King Chamber and sarcophagus in physical form, the Reiki hologram still offers energy that feels very similar to the real life experience, and can have a similar energetic effect.

You could also build on this process, inviting your Reiki crystal to then create Reiki holograms of gemstones and crystals placed on your physical body. Though it can be fun to work with for those who have a deep knowledge of the energetic properties of specific gemstones and crystals, that isn't actually necessary in order to perform this and have it be a powerful healing. The reason why is that there is Divine intelligence and Divine consciousness within your Reiki crystal, so simply asking your Reiki crystal to create a Reiki hologram of the most perfect gemstone and crystal healing will still work, without you having to specify the actual gemstone, crystal, or the individual healing properties of each. Do this now and notice the effect. Notice the energetic changes being caused through these many layers of light you are creating in the room and on and around your body through these advanced yet easy-to-use Reiki techniques.

Now, create Reiki holograms of specific angels to be present in the room. You may create Reiki holograms of various angels or many Reiki holograms of the same angel in various locations around the room. If, for example, you feel the need for wisdom during the session, you may want to create many Reiki holograms of the archangel Raziel to fill the space of the room with the energetic signature of that angel. Or, if you feel the need for protection, perhaps you would create many Reiki holograms of the archangel Michael. Again, these Reiki holograms simply replicate the energetic signature of the actual angel, which in itself can still greatly influence your own energy and consciousness in very positive ways.

Give yourself the freedom to play with these many possibilities when creating your own Reiki Temple of Divine Light. That temple is simply a deep layering of energetic signatures using a combination of Reiki portals and Reiki holograms, plus adding the Reiki Sphere of Divine Grace. Feel free to add your own variations if you prefer. Play with the options. Have fun.

CHAPTER TWELVE

The Reiki Sanctuary and The Reiki Sphere of Divine Grace

Most of my discoveries with Reiki happen spontaneously, when I am told by my guidance to try something new with Reiki. In my book *New Reiki Software for Divine Living* I explored the idea of a Reiki Sphere of Divine Grace, which is like a huge bubble made out of Reiki that your Reiki crystal can create around you or someone else. That bubble of Reiki light can be very soothing, and is a wonderful way to begin or end a Reiki session on yourself or others. You can experience this now by asking your Reiki crystal to create around you a Reiki Sphere of Divine Grace as follows:

I invite my Reiki crystal to create around me a Reiki Sphere of Divine Grace.

Once the Reiki Sphere of Divine Grace is created around you, something that happens instantly at your request, just allow yourself to be still inside of it for several minutes. Notice if you feel calmer or more relaxed while inside of this beautiful presence. I usually describe it as like being held in a place of deep nurturing by the Mother of the Universe.

Recently, while teaching at the Sivananda Ashram in the Bahamas, while on the beach one of my spirit guides told me to ask my Reiki crystal to put me into the Reiki Sanctuary. At first I resisted, because I didn't see how a Reiki Sanctuary would be any different than the loving, nurturing presence of being inside the Reiki Sphere of Divine Grace, so I ignored my guidance, which I foolishly do every now and then. Luckily, the voice persisted and again told me to ask my Reiki crystal to put me into the Reiki Sanctuary. So, I eventually listened to it and was amazed at what happened. Being in the Reiki Sanctuary felt very different than being in the Reiki Sphere of Divine Grace. It felt like I was in an energetic space that had a higher vibration than the Reiki Sphere of Divine Grace. When in the Reiki Sphere of Divine Grace I usually feel very relaxed, and when in the Reiki Sanctuary I feel more like I was in a very beautiful sacred space, like a church or other sacred space, which, although invoking a sense of serenity, is not the same as the deeply relaxed feeling of being in the Reiki Sphere of Divine Grace. Experience the Reiki Sanctuary now by asking your Reiki crystal:

I invite my Reiki crystal to put me into the Reiki Sanctuary.

Once inside the Reiki Sanctuary simply allow yourself to be still inside of it for several minutes. Notice if you feel energetically and mentally more clear, alert, or serene while inside of this beautiful presence. Note that the Reiki Sanctuary is different than the Reiki Temple of Divine Light, which is a far more involved process and also evokes a more intense level of energy than the Reiki Sanctuary.

CHAPTER THIRTEEN

Reiki Spinal Zap!

The sessions you have worked with so far, in one way or another, have been about connecting you deeper with the Divine, as well as with those angelic beings that support your healing and spiritual growth. This chapter still explores that Divine connection, but focuses more on how to work on that directly through the spine. If you wish for an intense experience of Reiki moving through the spine using the healing power of this book, simply keep reading the following paragraphs.

This book is now attuning your C-1 vertebra at the top of your spine to the Reiki of Yang, and the bones of your sacrum at the bottom of your spine to the Reiki of Yin. Close your eyes now and feel this flow of the Yin and Yang as it moves gently through your spine. As this flow continues, this book is now attuning each vertebra in your spine as a Reiki battery, and is running Reiki cords from each vertebra in your spine to every other vertebra, creating a thick web of Divine Reiki light throughout your spine. Now, this book is creating a Reiki portal in your spine to the archangel Raphael. Feel this angelic presence as it merges and flows throughout your being, emanating from the portal to Raphael existing now in your spine. Let yourself relax into this powerful flow of healing that is now moving through your entire spine.

Now, this book is creating a Reiki wave, rolling from the top of your spine all the way down to the base of your spine. Know that your karmic issues are often held in the karmic body, which is also near the spine. To release as much energetic debris as can be released, this book is now sending Lotus Reiki into your spine, since Lotus Reiki is a vibration of Reiki light designed to help release karmic issues. To amplify this effect, this book is now creating Lotus Reiki cords flowing through your karmic body from this moment in time, all the way back through all of your lifetimes, and back to that moment when you first separated as an individual soul from the Divine. This book is adding to that more Lotus Reiki cords, each flowing through every individual karmic issue held in your karmic body, from the moment that issue first was created in whichever lifetime, up through all your lifetimes, and into the present moment. Sit still in this energy, breathing slowly into it. Just close your eyes and allow your mind to empty as the Reiki energy releases all that it can release that is ready to be moved from your karmic body, releasing it to the Divine.

Now, this book is surrounding you with a Reiki Sphere of Divine Grace. Surrender into this ball of Divine light that is now surrounding you. Allow it to hold you with a sense of deep comfort and nurturing.

The Reiki crystal inside of this book is now drawing each cell of your spine into a deep Reiki meditation to radiate Divine love. Know this sense of love as it flows through each cell in each vertebra of your spine.

Know that the intensity of this Reiki spinal zap session is best experienced only in short intervals. So, now, the Reiki crystal inside of this book is dissolving and releasing all Reiki cords flowing through you, your karmic body, and your spine. These are now entirely released. Also, the Reiki crystal inside of this book is releasing the attunement of your C-1 vertebra to the Reiki of Yang and the attunement of your sacrum to the Reiki of Yin. These attunements are now entirely released. The Reiki crystal inside of this book is now creating a Reiki hologram of your spine in a state of perfect health, and is fusing that Reiki hologram into your physical spine for as long as is for your highest good.

This book is now sending you a Reiki integration session to assist in integrating all aspects of this healing, so that when the healing is fully finished you will feel refreshed, in touch with your body, and free from any residual energetic debris that was loosened from any issues held in your spine or karmic body. This book is also closing the Reiki portal in your spine to the archangel Raphael.

Now, this book is sending several Reiki waves simultaneously through your spine: one from the top down to the bottom and the other from the bottom up to the top of your spine. This cleansing light is washing any energetic residue from your spine.

Sit quietly now in stillness. Imagine your spine going all the way down into the center of the earth, rooting you and connecting you with this planet, this powerful being upon which we all live. Imagine your breath going all the way down, down through your lungs, through your spine, all the way down into the earth, and then back up again. Remember, the spine is the pillar that connects you to heaven and earth. Feel this connection as you breathe into it. Know you can engage this healing anytime you wish simply by reading this chapter. For now, it is time to integrate, to know and remember that you are both a heavenly being of the spiritual realm as well as an earthly being in this world of form. You are both, simultaneously! And that is the beauty of being human.

CHAPTER FOURTEEN

Reiki Family Constellation Session

One of the newest and more advanced techniques I have been shown with Reiki is something called a Reiki family constellation session. It is inspired by an alternative form of psychotherapy developed by Bert Hellinger called *family constellations*, which I highly recommend to any spiritual seeker or anyone interested in a deeper understanding of how the history or our family members and ancestors influences our psychological wellbeing today. What I love about the work of family constellation therapy is that it truly addresses the subconscious architecture of a family's group consciousness, including ancestors as well as present-day relatives. My experience with family constellation work showed me that the conscious and unconscious desires, needs, expectations, and emotions of all of our family members act as a collective energy, which is not amorphous or generic, but actually very specific in how it influences us.

What a Reiki family constellation session does is work on the streams of energy that influence us from our present-day family members as well as ancestors, and allow us to come to a place of inner peace with them. It came to me as a technique shortly after my son Dylan was born. Although he is a beautiful boy, and my wife and I love him dearly, immediately after his birth we began fighting as a couple. It seemed strange to me, since we didn't fight much at all in our twelve years as a couple before his birth. By tuning in deeper to what was going on, and having experienced family constellation work before, I realized that the subconscious patterns of both of our family systems were the real cause of our disputes. Neither my wife nor I are very close to our parents, and so in one sense it seemed we should have been immune to these kinds of influences, and yet here we were playing out dysfunctional roles that had been engraved into the subconscious architecture of our family systems. It was truly from a place of desperation that one day I asked my Reiki crystal to send a family constellation session to the situation, and immediately I began feeling better, as well as simultaneously aware of the influence of the spirit of my mother (who died a few years ago), the influence of my wife's living mother, the influences of my father, her father, and both of our grandparents; all this clutter of energy now involved in the situation surrounding the birth of our new son. Once I began sending this form of session, the dynamics of my relationship with my wife shifted in a profound way, back toward a relationship based on mutual respect.

You can experience a Reiki family constellation session yourself simply by asking your Reiki crystal to send you one. What happens is a bit hard to describe, but it feels to me almost like the Reiki crystal is creating Reiki holograms of a person's parents and ancestors the same way in a group therapy setting one picks others to represent members of their family, and that it is energetically moving those Reiki holograms around, the same way a family constellation therapist would ask members in the group field to reposition themselves until everyone in the group feels at peace. A Reiki family constellation session is quite different than just sending Reiki to a family situation or clearing the energetic cords between you and a family member, both of which are techniques I still recommend, given the circumstance.

Know just as with family constellation therapy you also can do Reiki constellation sessions related to issues outside of your family, such as work. Again, exactly what happens is a bit hard to describe, but the results are often amazing.

Here is the template for creating a Reiki family constellation session:

> *I invite my Reiki crystal to send a Reiki family constellation session to help resolve the following issue: (describe the problem).*

Your Reiki crystal does not need a time given for how long this session should go, since the session is going to happen at its own organic pace. Just ask for the session, and then surrender to the outcome. You will not be receiving Reiki directly from your Reiki crystal, nor will any of your family members or ancestors. The best way to think of it is that the Divine consciousness within the Reiki crystal is doing a kind of therapy session with your higher self, using Reiki holograms of the individual members of your family or that specific constellation to resolve the issue on the higher planes of reality. Know you can also use this session to help others. If you are sending a Reiki family constellation session to someone else's family, you need to have permission of at least one member of that family. It is always important to honor the free will of others and not interfere with their own spiritual evolution. So, please only use this session if a person has given permission for your energetic assistance. Once you have permission, the below template is what you would use:

I invite my Reiki crystal to send a Reiki family constellation session to (name of person) to help resolve the following issue: (describe the problem).

This session is now one of my favorite Reiki tools. Use it regularly for yourself and for others when permission is given.

CHAPTER FIFTEEN

Reiki DNA Blueprint Upgrade

The Reiki DNA blueprint upgrade is another new energetic session, and one I highly recommend. What happens is that the Reiki crystal is sending Reiki directly into your DNA to raise your energetic vibration at the genetic level. This may seem like an unnecessary adjustment to make, since our DNA is often thought of as being something that is fixed or permanent. Yet much new research about DNA shows that there are markers in our DNA code that can be triggered under certain circumstances. This is how spices like turmeric aid in the battle against cancer, by triggering latent aspects of DNA code that already exist. So, when doing a DNA blueprint upgrade, don't think that it's going to change your DNA in the sense of growing wings or an extra finger. It is merely energetically triggering what already exists so that the DNA is spiritually performing at an optimum level.

I have done such sessions on my son Dylan, and though I do not think these sessions can take full credit for him being such a magical and healthy little boy, I do think they are a contributing factor. Each time we take him in for his check-ups at the pediatrician they say he is *exceptionally* healthy. They say he is more alert than other babies his age, stronger, and beautiful. The compliments seem endless. Again, much of that can also be attributed to how he was cared for while in the womb: the nurturing diet his mother had and all the love she and I both gave to him while he was developing in utero. But, I do think the energy healing sessions have also been a part of the equation that has made him so *exceptionally* healthy.

Try this session on yourself now to experience it by following the template below:

> *I invite my Reiki crystal to send me a Reiki DNA blueprint upgrade session now.*

Then, sit back and relax and allow the session to fill all the DNA in all of your cells with this Divine Reiki light. To send such a session to another person, simply adapt the above phrase as follows:

I invite my Reiki crystal to send (name of the person) a Reiki DNA blueprint upgrade session now.

Using this type of session on yourself or others is highly recommended. You can incorporate it into more layered advanced sessions, which are shown in the chapters that follow.

CHAPTER SIXTEEN

Creating Your Own
Reiki Affirmations

Affirmations are positive phrases one can easily repeat
to change their mental programming about a specific
life issue. Made popular by the author Louise Hay, most
affirmations work on the concept that once we change
a thought pattern through repeated linguistic programming, our lives will similarly change for the better. What
we think is what we create. A Reiki affirmation, however,
addresses the issue not only by changing the mental pattern through linguistic programming, but also by sending
Reiki to the issue simultaneously. How this works is that
the Reiki affirmation is empowered with its own Reiki
crystal, which then is programmed to send Reiki to any-

one who says the affirmation for the duration of the time they are saying it.

My book *New Reiki Software for Divine Living* reveals twenty-two powerful Reiki affirmations that anyone can use, whether or not they are attuned to Reiki on any level. The reason this works is because the Reiki crystal within the affirmation itself is the Reiki practitioner. The Reiki crystal inside the affirmation is sending and directing the focus of the Reiki session. These sessions are designed to last only as long as the period of time when one is saying the affirmation, so that a person is inspired to keep repeating the affirmation, which helps to change their mental programming. Below is a Reiki affirmation you can repeat to yourself just to get a sense of how they work.

I am one with Divine love. I am one with Divine love. I am one with Divine love.

Repeat the phrase aloud or semi-audibly, so that your lips are actually moving and you are doing more than just thinking the words. Say the affirmation over and over for at least a minute to get the full energetic impact, though you can certainly do this longer if you wish.

Using Reiki affirmations is a great and easy way to be able to do Reiki in very user-friendly way. They are different from full Reiki sessions in that they are not so powerful that you are likely to fall asleep or go into a deep alpha wave while doing them, which can happen in full-blown Reiki sessions. This flexible nature of the Reiki affirmation allows you to be able to do them at work, at home when doing household chores, even when taking a walk or driving to the store. A wonderful thing about Reiki affirmations as well is that you can create your own to assist you on any life issue you might be working on.

Create your own Reiki affirmation by first deciding what you want to achieve through the Reiki affirmation. Do you want to have a deeper sense of self love? Do you want more prosperity? Do you want to feel a greater sense of who you truly are? Decide first what the purpose of your Reiki affirmation should be. Then, ask your Reiki crystal to bring you into a Reiki meditation to discover the best Reiki affirmation for your purpose. Usually this will take less than a minute, as your Reiki crystal will psychically give you a sense of what the best words are for this affirmation. Know that it isn't required to ask your Reiki crystal to do this. Some people who are good with words might write an affirmation quite easily, but I have often found that the Reiki crystal can point your consciousness to the best choice of words, so I recommend trying this technique at least once. When you have your affirmation, write it out on a piece of paper. Then, ask your Reiki crystal to empower that affirmation with its own Reiki crystal. This will take a few minutes, as the Reiki crystal inside your energetic field makes a replica of itself inside the combination of words that are the affirmation. Once this process is complete, tune in and try to sense the Reiki crystal inside of the Reiki affirmation. In order for the affirmation to work appropriately as a Reiki affirmation, you have to program the Reiki crystal using your thoughts. Imagine your psychic connection to this Reiki crystal that is inside of the Reiki affirmation, and simply intend that your thoughts are going into that Reiki crystal and telling it to send Reiki to anyone who says the affirmation while they are saying it. Feel your thoughts literally going into that Reiki crystal. Then, mentally hold the intention that whatever style of Reiki works best for this affirmation is the Reiki that will be sent. By this I mean that there are many variables and possibilities within Reiki, and the Reiki crystal can access all of these. So, intend that the Reiki crystal will pick those energetic possibilities that are in the greatest alignment with the Reiki affirmation. Send those thoughts into the Reiki crystal inside the Reiki affirmation, and then simply let go and know your work is done.

Now, practice saying your new Reiki affirmation aloud. The first time you create your own Reiki affirmation you might feel inclined to create several. Feel free to create as many as you wish, as long as you intend to make use of them personally or share them with friends and family.

CHAPTER SEVENTEEN

Reiki Crystal Healing Grid

The term "crystal grid" is often used in Reiki, most commonly to refer to a layout of physical crystals and sometimes gemstones changed with Reiki to assist a Reiki healer in their distant healing work. However, there is an adaptation of this technique that the Reiki cystal can offer, which I beleive is far more powerful and does not require any physical crystals at all. It instead involves a unified field of more than one Reiki crystal working in harmony toward the desired healing goal. That could be a collection of people who have all been empowered to their own Reiki crystal. You could also empower physical items, such as quartz crystals, healing stones, even living beings, such as plants or trees, with their own Reiki crystal, and then invite them to work together as a unified whole. Any of the above options would work. But, for the sake of simplicity, a Reiki crystal grid has been created within this book and exists on the following page.

Each of the images on the following page is empowered with its own Reiki crystal, and they are programmed to work as a functioning Reiki crystal healing grid for anyone who reads this book. These Reiki crystals also link up energetically with the Reiki crytsal inside of this book. You can call upon this Reiki crystal healing grid anytime you wish or need to by simply asking your Reiki crystal to connect with it. Once you do, the healing power available to you will increase exponentially.

Let's demonstrate the healing power of this grid by first having the book send you a healing using this Reiki crystal healing grid. Read the paragraph below and experience this level of healing.

The Reiki crystal inside this book is linking with the Reiki crystal healing grid from this book and sending you a healing now as you read this paragraph. As you continue reading, you may feel an intense flow of Reiki energy moving along your spine, filling your entire being with the Divine light known as Reiki. This healing is now focusing on the primary issue that you most need to resolve right now in this moment of your life, even if you do not know what that is. Continue reading and know that the Reiki crystal healing grid is working on that issue. As you keep on reading, now invite your own Reiki crystal to join this work. Quietly with your mind, simply ask your own Reiki crystal to link with this grid and to join in the healing. You might notice a slight increase in the flow of energy, or you might not. The important thing is that you are learning how to connect your own Reiki crystal with this crystal healing grid telepathically. Anytime that you wish, from this moment forward, you can simply ask your Reiki crystal to connect with the Reiki crystal healing grid, and it will.

Now, go back to the following page, the one with the empowered images, and stare at the page for as long as you wish this healing to continue. If you wish, you can even make a copy of that grid and it will still carry the same power. Post it on your wall at home, and use it as a healing image that is there for you anytime you need it. But, for it to work, you need to have read this paragraph and have linked your own Reiki crystal to this grid; that way an innocent person who simply walks by and glances at the image will not be sent a healing that they have not consented to.

It is important to remember as well that you can link to this crystal grid through your own Reiki crystal, and that this can be done distantly if you don't have a copy of the book with you. To do this, simply use the following template:

I invite my Reiki crystal to link with the Reiki crystal healing grid to send Reiki to (name of person or situation) for the next (name how many) minutes.

The power of the Reiki crystal grid can be quite intense, so I recommend using it primarily for situations or issues that need an energetic bolt of lightning to blast through the toughest and most difficult energetic obstacles.

CHAPTER EIGHTEEN

Advanced Psychic Reiki Sessions

Advanced Psychic Reiki can include any combination of the techniques explored from Chapter 6 though Chapter 18 of this book. I recommend working with each of those techniques until you have a deep intuitive understanding of how they impact you. Only use them on yourself first, and then, once you feel confident with each technique, begin to share them when offering Psychic Reiki sessions to others. Below are some suggested advanced Psychic Reiki sessions. Know that you are truly only limited by your imagination when working on yourself, and the free will consent of another person when working on them. The following advanced sessions are not intended to be the end all and be all of what is possible, but more suggestions intended to inspire you to come up with your own advanced sessions as well. Know that each of these sessions can be used as a self session or as a session on another person.

Karmic Release Session

Karma is the cumulative energetic residue of our past actions, beliefs, and emotions. Sometimes this idea can be oversimplified to mean that if you stole from someone in this life that they, or someone else, will steal from you. That oversimplification can lead us to misunderstand the many varied ways in which our karma can impact us. True, if you steal from someone that does create negative karma, but how and when that karma will play out can be in a variety of ways. It might show up as an illness, a missed opportunity, being isolated or lonely, or myriad other ways. The universe can be very creative in how and when that karma will play out. Also, karma does not have to be negative. We can have positive karma, as well as karma about learning a life lesson. If you did something really horrible in this life, or another life, most likely that karma will not be released by simply doing an energy healing, as something that deep would likely require a deeper level of atonement. But, there are situations where by bringing enough Divine light into our karmic conditioning we can release repetitious karmic patterns that may be unhealthy for us, or others. Many of these kinds of karmic issues can be entirely released through energy healing by performing a karmic release session. Depending on how deep the issue is, sometimes it may take more than one session. Also know there are those instances when a soul's karmic lessons require an issue be in place, and in those instances no amount of energy healing will change that. But, in many cases, energy healing for karmic release can make a profound difference in people's lives.

This Psychic Reiki Karmic Release session involves using a line of Reiki light I call Lotus Reiki, which is directly used for karmic release. There is a Reiki symbol one can use for Lotus Reiki, which is explored in my book *Reiki for Spiritual Healing*. However, since the Reiki crystal bypasses the need for any symbols, you can access this energy simply by asking your Reiki crystal to do so.

Begin the session by creating your own Reiki Temple of Divine Light as shown in Chapter 12, which will take several minutes. Once that is created, continue by asking your Reiki crystal to create a Reiki Sphere of Divine Grace as follows:

> *I invite my Reiki crystal to create a Reiki Sphere of Divine Grace around me (or person being treated). I ask that this remain in place for the entire session.*

Once the Reiki Sphere of Divine Grace is in place, invoke the following:

I invite my Reiki crystal to create Lotus Reiki cords through my karmic body from the present moment in time backwards to the moment of my (or person's name if working on another person) first incarnation. I ask that this remain in place for the next five minutes.

I do not recommend leaving these cords in place for longer than five minutes because the level of release for some people can be quite extreme if left for too long. While the Reiki cords are still in place, invoke the following:

I invite my Reiki crystal to send Lotus Reiki to my (or other person's) karmic body, mental body, emotional body, spiritual body, and all my organs and organ systems. I ask that this remain in place for the next twenty minutes.

While the Lotus Reiki is flowing through all these, as well as through the timeline of the karmic body, invoke the following to deepen the healing even more:

I invite my Reiki crystal to bring me (or other person) into a Reiki meditation to know the love the Divine has for me (or that person). I ask that this Reiki meditation remain in place for the next twenty minutes.

Deepen the session even more by continuing to layer in more techniques simultaneously while Reiki is still flowing through all these. Invoke the following:

> *I invite my Reiki crystal to create a Reiki portal to the Divine inside of my (or other person's) spine and karmic body. I ask that this Reiki portal remain in place for the next twenty minutes.*

Continue to deepen the session with more layering techniques. Invoke the following:

> *I invite my Reiki crystal to create a Reiki hologram of my (or other person's) karmic body free from any major karmic issues, and to infuse this Reiki hologram into my (or other person's) karmic body now. I ask that this Reiki hologram remain for as long as is for the highest good.*

Allow this layered session to run unaltered until the five minute mark. Then, once the first five minutes have been reached, release the Reiki cords that were invoked early during the session by saying the following:

> *I invite my Reiki crystal to release the Lotus Reiki cords that were created through my karmic body from the present moment in time backwards to the moment of my (or person's name if working on another person) first incarnation. I ask for this now.*

Follow this by asking your Reiki crystal to create a Reiki sieve, and move it along the timeline of the person's existence, from their first incarnation to the present moment. A Reiki sieve is an energetic mesh device made out of Reiki by the Reiki crystal that will catch and remove any energetic debris that was released from the karmic body, but which may still be lingering in a person's energy field. This simple technique is one I only use during these karmic sessions, which is why I did not devote an entire chapter to Reiki sieves. However, I have found using them is extraordinary in terms of allowing a person to feel more integrated at the end of an intense session for karmic release. Invoke a Reiki sieve by saying the following to your Reiki crystal:

> *I invite my Reiki crystal to create a Reiki sieve and move it through my (or other person's) karmic body from the moment of my (or person's name if working on another person) first incarnation through all of their lifetimes up to the present moment, lifting all energetic debris up sixty feet above me (or other person) and back to the Divine where it is fully transformed and released.*

Once the Reiki cords are released and the Reiki sieve has removed all related energetic debris, allow the remaining layered Reiki session to run unaltered for the next fifteen minutes. Then, begin to bring the session to a close with the following:

> *I invite my Reiki crystal to shift all the lines of light that it has been sending now to be for the most gentle and most perfect form of integration. I ask for this now.*

Once the Reiki integration process begins, the energy itself may begin to feel heavier or denser to the one receiving it. This is because the integration lines of light are designed to remind us of our physical self. You can add to this process by adding the following techniques to bring the session to an even gentler and more pleasant closure:

> *I invite my Reiki crystal to create a Reiki grounding cord from my (or other person's) root chakra all the way down to the center of the Earth. I ask that this remain in place until it is no longer needed.*

Follow this by asking your Reiki crystal to create Reiki holograms of something pleasant, such as flowers, covering the recipient's body from head to toe:

> *I invite my Reiki crystal to create Reiki holograms of a thousand red rose petals covering me (or other person) from head to toe. I ask that these remain in place until they are no longer needed.*

The Reiki crystal will usually bring the Reiki integration process to a close within five minutes. The exact amount of time it takes will vary depending on the person's energy system and how deep the session was. Once you sense the session is complete, drink plenty of water to assist the cells of your body and your kidneys in further releasing any toxins that may have been moved out at the cellular level by the session.

PSYCHIC REIKI

Mental/Emotional Clearing Session

Traditional Reiki offers a symbol called Sei He Ki, which is wonderful to use for mental/emotional healing. Since the Reiki crystal accesses all Reiki symbols, know that the energy of Sei He Ki will be part of any request you make to the Reiki crystal for mental/emotional healing. Also, the Psychic Reiki session can take things a step further in releasing the built-in mental/emotional patterns that often contribute to or are the root cause of mental/emotional issues through the added techniques such as Reiki affirmations, Reiki holograms, the Reiki crystal grid, and more.

Begin the session by creating your own Reiki Temple of Divine Light as shown in Chapter Twelve. Once that is created, continue as follows:

> *I invite my Reiki crystal to create a Reiki Sphere of Divine Grace around (name of person). I ask that this remain in place for the entire session.*

Follow this by asking your Reiki crystal to open a Reiki portal to the angelic realm, six inches above, as follows:

> *I invite my Reiki crystal to create a Reiki portal to the angelic realm (specify particular angel if you wish) six inches above (name of person's) crown chakra. I ask that this remain in place for the entire session.*

Follow this by asking your Reiki crystal to create a Reiki hologram of your brain and nervous system in the most perfect state of serenity, as follows:

> *I invite my Reiki crystal to create a Reiki hologram of (name of person's) brain and nervous system in a state of perfect health and serenity, and to fuse that Reiki hologram in with (name of person's) brain and nervous system for as long as is for the highest good.*

Follow this by asking your Reiki crystal to connect with the Reiki crystal healing grid inside this book (which it can do distantly) and to activate a Reiki crystal healing grid session on your mental body and emotional body, as follows:

> *I invite my Reiki crystal to link with the Reiki crystal healing grid to send Reiki to (name of person's) mental body and emotional body for the next twenty minutes.*

Given the strength of the Reiki crystal healing grid, it is important to monitor the person receiving the healing to make sure they do not become overwhelmed. If they do become overwhelmed, or if you become overwhelmed while doing this session on yourself, feel free to end this aspect of the healing sooner than the twenty minutes by simply asking your Reiki crystal to discontinue using the Reiki crystal healing grid in that session. You can also ask the Reiki crystal to release the session backwards in time at the moment it began if the person, or you, are exhibiting any signs of a deep healing crisis—where unresolved issues rise to the surface of a person's awareness faster than they are capable of processing emotionally.

However, the amount of energetic clearing that can happen to both the mental body and emotional body in using this technique is tremendous. And, in the vast majority of cases, most people can process it. So, use the technique and know you can release it and change course if there is any sense of overwhelm arising during the session. To continue going deeper with the session you can add another layer to the healing by invoking the following:

> *I invite my Reiki crystal to bring (name of person's) mind into a Reiki meditation for stillness and inner peace for the next twenty minutes.*

Allow this layered session to run its course for twenty minutes (unless you have to end it early as mentioned before). Once the twenty-minute session is complete, ask your Reiki crystal to end the session with the following:

> *I invite my Reiki crystal to shift all the lines of light that it has been sending to now be for the most gentle and most perfect form of integration. I ask for this now.*

Remember, once the Reiki integration process begins, the energy itself may begin to feel heavier or denser to the one receiving it, because the integration lines of light are designed to remind us of our physical self. You can deepen this process by adding the following techniques to bring the session to an even gentler and more pleasant closure:

> *I invite my Reiki crystal to create a Reiki grounding cord from my (or other person's) root chakra all the way down to the center of the Earth. I ask that this remain in place until it is no longer needed.*

Follow this by asking your Reiki crystal to create Reiki holograms of something pleasant, such as flowers, covering the recipient's body from head to toe:

> *I invite my Reiki crystal to create Reiki holograms of a thousand pink carnations covering me (or other person) from head to toe. I ask that these remain in place until they are no longer needed.*

The Reiki crystal will usually bring the Reiki integration process to a close within five minutes. The exact amount of time it takes depends on the person's energy system and how deep the session was. Once you sense that the session is complete, drink plenty of water to assist the cells of your body and your kidneys in further releasing any toxins that may have been moved out at the cellular level by the session.

Organ~Specific Sessions

It is very common for a Reiki practitioner to be asked to offer a session related to a specific organ or organ system in the body. The following are general guidelines you can use to offer a Reiki session for almost any organ or organ system. Remember as well that Reiki is not intended to be a substitute for medical care, yet it is often a wonderful compliment to any form of healing.

Begin the session by creating your own Reiki Temple of Divine Light as shown in Chapter Twelve. Once that is created, continue as follows:

> *I invite my Reiki crystal to create a Reiki Sphere of Divine Grace around (name of person). I ask that this remain in place for the entire session.*

Continue the session by asking your Reiki crystal to send Reiki to all the organs and organ systems in the body. Even though you want to focus on a specific organ, the greater benefit will happen if this is in conjunction with a Reiki session for the entire body. So, begin the session as follows:

> *I invite my Reiki crystal to send Reiki to (name of person's) brain and nervous system, circulatory system, lymphatic system, digestive system, respiratory system, muscular system, skeletal system, and all glands and all*

organs of the body. I ask that this continue for the next twenty minutes (you can specify longer if need be).

Keep layering the session by asking your Reiki crystal to send Reiki to all the chakras and meridian systems in the body as follows:

I invite my Reiki crystal to send Reiki to (name of person's) chakras and meridian system, to release any energetic debris that is an obstacle to their highest health and highest good.

Continue layering the session even deeper by asking your Reiki crystal to send Reiki to all the energetic bodies as follows:

I invite my Reiki crystal to send Reiki to (name of person's) mental body, etheric body, emotional body, spiritual body, and karmic body system to release any energetic debris that is an obstacle to their highest health and highest good. I ask that this continue for the next twenty minutes (you can specify longer if need be).

Once the layering of the session is fully in place focus on the specific organ or organ system that needs extra attention by asking your Reiki crystal to send Reiki cords through that organ or organ system, as follows:

I invite my Reiki crystal to create Reiki cords through the timeline of (name person's organ or organ system) from the present moment backwards in time to the moment of their birth. I ask that this continue for the next twenty minutes (you can specify longer if need be).

If you are good with anatomy and a sense of geometric/special relationships, you can at this point amplify the session by also running new Reiki cords through the organ or organ system by attaching those cords between two points in close proximity to the organ or organ system in question. For example, I often run Reiki cords from the left side of my rib cage to the right side of my rib cage when needing a strong dose of Reiki through my lungs. This technique is entirely optional since it would require a decent knowledge of human anatomy and will vary greatly depending on the organ or organ system in question. Still, I do recommend it for those willing to explore this option.

Now, continue layering the session even deeper by asking your Reiki crystal to create Reiki holograms of the organ or organ system in a state of perfect health, and to infuse that Reiki hologram into the real organ or organ system as follows:

I invite my Reiki crystal to create Reiki holograms of the (name person's organ or organ system) in a state of perfect health and to infuse that Reiki hologram into (name person's organ or organ system). I ask that this continue for as long as is for the person's highest good.

Since Reiki holograms can remain in place long after a session has ended, do not specify their end time, but instead simply leave it open-ended to be for their highest good. With time the Reiki holograms will eventually fade out, but they may remain in place for minutes or even hours after the session is complete.

Further deepen the layering process by asking your Reiki crystal to bring each cell of that organ or organ system into a Reiki meditation, so that the consciousness of each cell emanates perfect health, as follows:

> *I invite my Reiki crystal to bring the consciousness in each cell of the (name person's organ or organ system) into a Reiki meditation to emanate a state of perfect health in that (name person's organ or organ system). I ask that this continue for as long as is for the highest good.*

Complete the layering process by asking your Reiki crystal to include the Reiki crystal healing grid as follows:

> *I invite my Reiki crystal to link with the Reiki crystal healing grid to send Reiki to (name person's organ or organ system) for the next twenty minutes*

Allow the session now to run its course, making minor adjustments as need be if you feel inspired to bring in Reiki portals to the angelic realm, create Reiki holograms of angels, or anything that adds an extra touch to the session.

Once the session has run its course, bring it to a close as follows:

> *I invite my Reiki crystal to shift all the lines of light that it has been sending to now be for the most gentle and most perfect form of integration. I ask for this now.*

Remember, as the Reiki integration process begins, the energy itself may begin to feel denser to the one receiving it. I recommend mentioning this if the session is on another person so that they do not panic when sensing the dense or heavy energy, which some people do when not told about it in advance. Then add to this process by using the following techniques to bring the session to an even gentler and more pleasant closure:

> *I invite my Reiki crystal to create a Reiki grounding cord from my (or other person's) root chakra all the way down to the center of the Earth. I ask that this remain in place until it is no longer needed.*

Follow this by asking your Reiki crystal to create Reiki holograms of something pleasant, such as flowers, covering the recipient's body from head to toe:

> *I invite my Reiki crystal to create Reiki holograms of a thousand yellow daisies covering me (or other person) from head to toe. I ask that these remain in place until they are no longer needed.*

The Reiki crystal will usually bring the Reiki integration process to a close within five minutes. The exact amount of time it takes depends on the person's energy system and how deep the session was. Once you sense the session is complete, drink plenty of water to assist the cells of your body and your kidneys in further releasing any toxins that may have been moved out at the cellular level by the session.

Session for Stress Release

Stress is an unfortunate product of our fast-paced world. It is also an underlying factor in many serious medical conditions, such as high blood pressure, asthma, and heart disease. Though it is hard to imagine living a life entirely free of stress, being able to limit stress and release it when it is present is a powerful benefit of working with your Reiki crystal. The following stress-release technique can be used on yourself or others, and can be quite beneficial if used on a regular basis.

Begin the session by creating your own Reiki Temple of Divine Light as shown in Chapter Twelve. Once that is created, continue as follows:

> *I invite my Reiki crystal to create a Reiki Sphere of Divine Grace around (name of person). I ask that this remain in place for the entire session.*

Add a deeper level of emotional safety by invoking the Reiki Sanctuary as follows:

I invite my Reiki crystal to create a Reiki Sanctuary around (name of person). I ask that this remain in place for the entire session.

Follow this by asking your Reiki crystal to open a Reiki portal to the angelic realm, six inches above, as follows:

I invite my Reiki crystal to create a Reiki portal to the angelic realm (specify particular angel if you wish) six inches above (name of person's) crown chakra. I ask that this remain in place for the entire session.

Follow this by asking your Reiki crystal to create a Reiki hologram of the archangel Raphael with his hands on the shoulders of the person being treated, as follows:

I invite my Reiki crystal to create a Reiki hologram of the archangel Raphael with his hands on (name of person's) shoulders for comfort and healing. I ask that this remain in place for the entire session.

Continue the session by asking your Reiki crystal to create Reiki cords through the entire muscular system, from the present time all the way back to the moment of birth as follows:

> *I invite my Reiki crystal to create Reiki cords through (name of person's) muscular system and each individual muscle, tendon, and ligament from present time backwards to the moment of birth. I ask that this continue for the next twenty minutes.*

Deepen the session by asking your Reiki crystal to invoke a Reiki meditation for release of all stress and tension at the cellular level:

> *I invite my Reiki crystal to bring the consciousness in each cell holding stress and tension in (name of person's) body into a Reiki meditation to emanate a state of perfect health and to know freedom from all tension and stress. I ask that this continue for as long as is for the highest good.*

Layer the session even more by asking your Reiki crystal to send Reiki to the root issue that is causing the stress:

> *I invite my Reiki crystal to send Reiki to the root issue causing stress for (name of person). I ask that this continue for the next twenty minutes.*

Continue the session by asking your Reiki crystal to create a Reiki hologram of the person free from stress or tension and to merge that Reiki hologram into their physical body as follows:

I invite my Reiki crystal to create a Reiki hologram of (name of person) that is free from all tension and stress, then to merge that Reiki hologram in with their physical body. I ask that this continue for as long as is for their highest good.

Add to the session even more by asking your Reiki crystal to cleanse the meridians of any energetic obstacles causing stress:

I invite my Reiki crystal to send Reiki through the energy meridians of (name of person) to clear them from all tension and stress. I ask that this continue for the next twenty minutes.

Include even more Reiki cords in the session by asking your Reiki crystal to send Reiki cords through the chakras to release all energies that may be causing tension and stress:

I invite my Reiki crystal to create Reiki cords through (name of person's) chakra system and each individual chakra from present time backwards to the moment of birth. I ask that this continue for the next twenty minutes.

Wait twenty minutes so those aspects of the healing designed to run for twenty minutes can come to completion, then ask your Reiki crystal to perform a Healing Emanation as follows:

> *I ask my Reiki crystal to create a Reiki holograms of my hands and to place these Reiki holograms on (name of person's) belly, performing Healing Emanation for the next ten minutes.*

Allow this to continue for approximately ten minutes, allowing the Healing Emanation aspect of the session to marinate in the person's body, mind, and spirit. Once the ten minutes have come to an end, shift toward closure and integration as follows:

> *I invite my Reiki crystal to shift all the lines of light that it has been sending to now be for the most gentle and most perfect form of integration. I ask for this now.*

Then add to this process by using the following techniques to bring the session to an even gentler and more pleasant closure:

> *I invite my Reiki crystal to create a Reiki grounding cord from (name of person's) root chakra all the way down to the center of the Earth. I ask that this remain in place until it is no longer needed.*

Follow this by asking your Reiki crystal to create Reiki holograms of something pleasant, such as flowers, covering the recipient's body from head to toe:

I invite my Reiki crystal to create Reiki holograms of a thousand poppies covering (name of person) from head to toe. I ask that these remain in place until they are no longer needed.

The Reiki crystal will usually bring the Reiki integration process to a close within five minutes. The exact amount of time it takes depends on the person's energy system and how deep the session was. Once you sense the session is complete, drink plenty of water.

Session for Cutting Negative Energy Cords

Energy healers and shamans know that our energy field plays an important role in our physical, mental, and spiritual health. If negative energy manifests in your field, that can often play out as a negative thought, emotion, or even physical illness. However, that negative energy can sometimes be coming from someone else, or something else. Cutting the negative energy cords between you and any source of negativity can often be an important step toward moving into true freedom and being in charge of you own energy field, as opposed to being a victim of the thoughts and emotions of those around you. If you ever have been in a dysfunctional romantic relationship, dysfunctional work relationship, or simply at the effect of the negative energy of someone else, you know how that can impact you in ways that are not for your highest good. The technique that follows is for clearing energy cords *between* you and another. The session is simply designed to cut the cord before it enters your energy field. Therefore the original source of the cord does not need be asked or have given consent for to this session to happen.

Start the session by creating your own Reiki Temple of Divine Light as shown in Chapter Twelve. Once that is created, continue as follows:

> *I invite my Reiki crystal to create a Reiki Sphere of Divine Grace around (name of person being healed). I ask that this remain in place for the entire session.*

Add a deeper level of emotional safety by invoking the Reiki Sanctuary as follows:

> *I invite my Reiki crystal to create a Reiki Sanctuary around (name of person being healed). I ask that this remain in place for the entire session.*

Follow this by asking your Reiki crystal to open a Reiki portal to the angelic realm to the archangel Michael, since he is the angel you would access for cutting away negative cords and negative energy. Do this six inches above the person's crown chakra, as follows:

> *I invite my Reiki crystal to create a Reiki portal to the archangel Michael six inches above (name of person's)*

crown chakra. I ask that this remain in place for the entire session.

Follow this by asking your Reiki crystal to create a Reiki hologram of the archangel Michael with his hands on the shoulders of the person being treated, as follows:

> *I invite my Reiki crystal to create a Reiki hologram of the archangel Michael with his hands on (name of person's) shoulders for protection and healing. I ask that this remain in place for the entire session.*

Now, ask your Reiki crystal to send the most powerful Reiki lights designed to cut energy cords by asking your Reiki crystal to send as follows:

> *I invite my Reiki crystal to send the highest and most powerful forms of Reiki to cut, release, dissolve, and transmute all energy cords not of the highest good between (name of person being healed) and (name of the source of the negative energy cord). I ask that this remain in place for the next twenty minutes, working on all levels and all dimensions of reality.*

Wait twenty minutes, allowing the healing to run its course. Know that after the twenty minutes you can repeat the above invocation again as many times as is needed to complete the cord clearing. Now, ask your Reiki crystal to send protective light as follows:

I invite my Reiki crystal to send the highest and most powerful forms of protective Reiki to protect (name of person being healed) from any negative, harmful, or unwanted energy from (name of the source of the energy cord). I ask that this remain in place for the next twenty minutes, working on all levels and all dimensions of reality.

Once the twenty minutes have come to an end, shift toward closure and integration as follows:

I invite my Reiki crystal to shift all the lines of light that it has been sending to now be for the most gentle and most perfect form of integration. I ask for this now.

Then add to this process by using the following techniques to bring the session to an even gentler and more pleasant closure:

I invite my Reiki crystal to create a Reiki grounding cord from (name of person's) root chakra all the way down to the center of the Earth. I ask that this remain in place until it is no longer needed.

Follow this by asking your Reiki crystal to create Reiki holograms of something pleasant, such as flowers, covering the recipient's body from head to toe:

I invite my Reiki crystal to create Reiki holograms of a thousand morning glories covering (name of person) from head to toe. I ask that these remain in place until they are no longer needed.

Allow the Reiki crystal to bring the Reiki integration process gently to a close, which usually takes five minutes or less. Once you sense the session is complete, the person who received the healing should drink plenty of water to assist in further releasing any toxins that may have been moved out at the cellular level by the session.

Be aware that many times people can be fully cleared of a negative cord, just to have it re-manifest again later in the days or weeks that follow. If that is happening, combine this session with both a karmic release session and a mental/emotional session, since it may be that the person has unresolved karma or an unresolved emotional issue related that is a root cause for creating this kind of drama. Knowing how and when to combine such sessions is an art that a practitioner will learn over time, with repeated practice. Those who need repeated cord cutting healings may be living out patterns of abuse from earlier in life, and can benefit from the session for healing abuse, which follows.

Session for Healing from Abuse

Physical, sexual, and emotional abuse can happen in many forms, and an unfortunately high percentage of people suffer from some type of abuse in their lives. For me personally, as an abuse survivor, I have found energy healing to be a primary key to overcoming a past that was riddled with severe trauma. Though other healing techniques were helpful, such as traditional psychotherapy and shamanic healing, it has been the consistent use of energy healing that has transformed my life from being someone who was a depressed loner to being a happy husband, father, and teacher who travels the world and is known for a loud and boisterous laugh. I rarely have a day now where I am in a bad mood, let alone depressed. I credit that shift to energy healing techniques, some of which are not Reiki-related but many of which are. The following technique will help release much of the energetic baggage that those who have suffered from any type of abuse often find to be an unwanted burden in their lives, and includes a similar cord cutting technique as the previous session, just that the overall focus is more designed to healing issues from the past.

Begin the session by creating your own Reiki Temple of Divine Light as shown in Chapter Twelve. Once that is created, continue as follows:

I invite my Reiki crystal to create a Reiki Sphere of Divine Grace around (name of person). I ask that this remain in place for the entire session.

Add a deeper level of emotional safety by invoking the Reiki Sanctuary as follows:

I invite my Reiki crystal to create a Reiki Sanctuary around (name of person). I ask that this remain in place for the entire session.

Follow this by asking your Reiki crystal to open a Reiki portal to the angelic realm, six inches above, as follows:

I invite my Reiki crystal to create a Reiki portal to the angelic realm (specify particular angel if you wish) six inches above (name of person's) crown chakra. I ask that this remain in place for the entire session.

Follow this by asking your Reiki crystal to create a Reiki hologram of the archangel Raphael with his hands on the shoulders of the person being treated, as follows:

I invite my Reiki crystal to create a Reiki hologram of the archangel Raphael with his hands on (name of person's) shoulders for comfort and healing. I ask that this remain in place for the entire session.

Once these initial steps of the session are fully in place, focus on releasing energetic attachments between the person you are working on and anyone who has abused them in their past. Do this by asking your Reiki crystal to send Reiki cords through the aka cords between them and anyone who has abused them. Aka cords are energetic cords between people that carry the energetic imprint of a relationship. Aka cords themselves are neither good nor bad, as they can exist in a positive sense between friends, lovers, and families and hold energy of kindness and love. But, in situations of abuse, these same cords often bind victims of abuse to their abuser emotionally, even long after they have left an abusive relationship or situation. Invoke this aka cords clearing as follows:

> *I invite my Reiki crystal to create Reiki cords through the timelines of all the aka cords between (name of person) and anyone who has abused them in this life or any other life, from the present moment backwards in time to the moment when each individual aka cord was formed between (name of person) and anyone who has abused them. I ask that this continue for the next twenty minutes (you can specify longer if need be).*

Follow this by asking your Reiki crystal to connect with the Reiki crystal healing grid inside this book (which it can do distantly) and to activate a Reiki crystal healing grid session on the person, as follows:

I invite my Reiki crystal to link with the Reiki crystal healing grid to send Reiki to (name of person) to release all forms of abuse held in their physical body, etheric body, mental body, emotional body, spiritual body, and karmic body for the next twenty minutes.

Follow this by asking your Reiki crystal to send Lotus Reiki to the person's karmic body to release any negative karma between them and any abusers, as follows:

I invite my Reiki crystal to send Lotus Reiki to (name of person's) karmic body to release all karmic conditioning related to the issue of abuse for the next twenty minutes.

Further deepen this layering process by asking your Reiki crystal to bring all cells in that person's body that are holding trauma from abuse into a Reiki meditation, so that the consciousness of each cell emanates perfect health and is free from all trauma, as follows:

I invite my Reiki crystal to bring the consciousness in each cell holding the trauma of abuse in (name of person's) body into a Reiki meditation to emanate a state of perfect health and know freedom from all trauma. I ask that this continue for the next twenty minutes.

From here allow the layered session to marinate in the person's body, mind, and spirit. Once the twenty minutes have come to an end, shift toward closure and integration as follows:

> *I invite my Reiki crystal to shift all the lines of light that it has been sending to now be for the most gentle and most perfect form of integration. I ask for this now.*

Then add to this process by using the following techniques to bring the session to an even gentler and more pleasant closure:

> *I invite my Reiki crystal to create a Reiki grounding cord from (name of person's) root chakra all the way down to the center of the Earth. I ask that this remain in place until it is no longer needed.*

Follow this by asking your Reiki crystal to create Reiki holograms of something pleasant, such as flowers, covering the recipient's body from head to toe:

> *I invite my Reiki crystal to create Reiki holograms of a thousand white rose petals covering (name of person) from head to toe. I ask that these remain in place until they are no longer needed.*

The Reiki crystal will usually bring the Reiki integration process to a close within five minutes, depending on the person's energy system and how deep the session was.

Once you sense the session is complete, invite the person being healed to drink plenty of water to assist in the release of any toxins that may have been moved out at the cellular level by the session.

You can also add in a remedy of ongoing Reiki affirmation exercises for the person as a follow-up practice. This is recommended for issues that are chronic and deeply ingrained in a person, which is often the case for those who are recovering from severe abuse. You can create one specific to the person and their abuse issues for them to use and repeat, or use one of these below:

> *I am whole, resilient, and vibrantly alive.*
> *I am whole, resilient, and vibrantly alive.*
> *I am whole, resilient, and vibrantly alive.*

> *I am pure, healed, and loved by the Divine.*
> *I am pure, healed, and loved by the Divine.*
> *I am pure, healed, and loved by the Divine*

> *I am joyful, happy, and free.*
> *I am joyful, happy, and free*
> *I am joyful, happy, and free*

Session for Healing Racial Bias

This session is one that I recommend for everyone. It is aimed not to just help those who have been victims of racial bias, but also is designed to root out an individual's own prejudices related to racial bias and thus help heal society as a whole. I am a firm believer that Reiki can transform not only our individual issues, but also heal our world at large. For too long the greater spiritual holistic healing community has remained silent on issues of race. If the wonderful tools we have, such as Reiki, can transform us as individuals, then they can also help heal some of society's greatest wounds. The healing below can be used for yourself, as well as for others, but does still require their consent. In other words, you cannot simply perform the session on someone who you feel is racist without their consent. Healing at this level requires the free will participation of the person being healed. However, in my own journey I have found that even the most well-meaning person can hold negative racial beliefs and stereotypes due to social conditioning. Often it is this unintended racial bias in the collective whole that prevents greater positive change from happening. So, even if you feel no real need to try this healing, try it anyway, as the benefits are likely to surprise you.

Begin the session by creating your own Reiki Temple of Divine Light as shown in Chapter Twelve. Once that is created, continue as follows:

> *I invite my Reiki crystal to create a Reiki Sphere of Divine Grace around (name of person). I ask that this remain in place for the entire session.*

Add a deeper level of emotional safety by invoking the Reiki Sanctuary as follows:

> *I invite my Reiki crystal to create a Reiki Sanctuary around (name of person). I ask that this remain in place for the entire session.*

Follow this by asking your Reiki crystal to open a Reiki portal to the angelic realm, six inches above, as follows:

> *I invite my Reiki crystal to create a Reiki portal to the angelic realm (specify particular angel if you wish) six inches above (name of person's) crown chakra. I ask that this remain in place for the entire session.*

Follow this by asking your Reiki crystal to create a Reiki hologram of the archangel Raphael with his hands on the shoulders of the person being treated, as follows:

> *I invite my Reiki crystal to create a Reiki hologram of the archangel Raphael with his hands on (name of person's) shoulders for comfort and healing. I ask that this remain in place for the entire session.*

Once these initial steps of the session are fully in place, ask your Reiki crystal to create a Reiki meditation to compassionately reveal any racial bias that is held at a subconscious level:

> *I invite my Reiki crystal to bring (name of person) into a Reiki meditation to reveal all negative social conditioning about race so that it can be witnessed and released. I ask that this remain in place for the next twenty minutes.*

Follow this by asking your Reiki crystal to create Reiki cords through the brain and nervous system to clear any negative social conditioning with regards to race:

> *I invite my Reiki crystal to create a Reiki cord through (name of person's) brain and nervous system from the present moment backwards in time to the moment of their birth, to clear and release all negative racial beliefs, negative racial belief systems, and negative racial thought forms. I ask that this remain in place for the next twenty minutes.*

Continue layering this session by asking your Reiki crystal to create Reiki holograms of the brain and nervous system free from any negative social conditioning with regards to race:

> *I invite my Reiki crystal to create Reiki holograms of (name of person's) brain and nervous system free from all negative social conditioning about race and to infuse this Reiki hologram into their brain and nervous system. I ask that this remain in place for as long as is for the highest good.*

Continue deepening the layering process by asking your Reiki crystal to send Reiki to the mental body to clear and release any negative racial conditioning:

> *I invite my Reiki crystal to send Reiki to (name of person's) mental body to release all negative social conditioning about race. I ask that this continue for the next twenty minutes.*

Further deepen this layering process by asking your Reiki crystal to bring all cells in that person's body that are holding racial trauma into a Reiki meditation, so that the consciousness of each cell emanates perfect health and is free from all racial trauma, as follows:

> *I invite my Reiki crystal to bring the consciousness in each cell holding racial trauma in (name of person's) body into a Reiki meditation to emanate a state of perfect health and know freedom from all racial trauma. I ask that this continue for the next twenty minutes.*

Now address any negative racial conditioning held at the karmic level by invoking the following:

> *I invite my Reiki crystal to create Lotus Reiki cords through (name of person's) karmic body from the present moment in time backwards to the moment of (name of person's) first incarnation. I ask that this remain in place for the next five minutes.*

I would not recommend leaving these cords in place for longer than five minutes since the level of release for some people can be quite extreme if left for too long. While the Reiki cords are still in place, invoke the following:

> *I invite my Reiki crystal to send Lotus Reiki to (name of person's) karmic body to release all negative racial karmic conditioning. I ask that this remain in place for the next twenty minutes.*

Deepen the session even more by continuing to layer in more techniques simultaneously while Reiki is still flowing through all these. Invoke the following:

> *I invite my Reiki crystal to create a Reiki portal to the Divine inside of (name of person's) spine and karmic body. I ask that this Reiki portal remain in place for the next twenty minutes.*

Continue to deepen the session with more layering techniques. Invoke the following:

> *I invite my Reiki crystal to create a Reiki hologram of my (or other person's) karmic body free from any racial karmic issues, and to infuse this Reiki hologram into my (or name of person's) karmic body now. I ask that this Reiki hologram remain for as long as is for the highest good.*

After five minutes, release all Reiki cords, but allow the remaining functions to continue, as follows:

> *I ask my Reiki crystal to release all Reiki cords through (name of person's) karmic body.*

Immediately follow by saying to your Reiki crystal:

> *I invite my Reiki crystal to create a Reiki sieve and move it through (name of person's) karmic body from the moment of (name of person's) first incarnation through all of their lifetimes up to the present moment, lifting all energetic debris up sixty feet above (person's name) and back to the Divine where it is fully transformed and released.*

Once the Reiki cords are released and the Reiki sieve has removed all related energetic debris, allow the remaining layered Reiki session to run unaltered for the next fifteen minutes. Then, begin to bring the session to a close with the following:

> *I invite my Reiki crystal to shift all the lines of light that it has been sending to now be for the most gentle and most perfect form of integration. I ask for this now.*

Then add to this process by using the following techniques to bring the session to an even gentler and more pleasant closure:

> *I invite my Reiki crystal to create a Reiki grounding cord from (name of person's) root chakra all the way down to the center of the Earth. I ask that this remain in place until it is no longer needed.*

Follow this by asking your Reiki crystal to create Reiki holograms of something pleasant, such as flowers, covering the recipient's body from head to toe:

> *I invite my Reiki crystal to create Reiki holograms of a thousand irises covering (name of person) from head to toe. I ask that these remain in place until they are no longer needed.*

The Reiki crystal will usually bring the Reiki integration process to a close within five minutes. The exact amount of time it takes depends on the person's energy system and how deep the session was. Once you sense the session is complete, invite the person being healed to drink plenty of water to assist the cells of their body and kidneys in further release of any toxins that may have been moved out at the cellular level by the session.

Session for Healing Gender Bias

The following session is quite similar to the previous one, and is also recommended for anyone whether or not they feel that they have any issues related to gender that need healing. The collective cultural blind spot we have, related to both race and gender, is so huge that many well-intentioned people have enormous issues that they cannot see, nor admit to, for the very fabric of our society is woven to make these issues seem as though they do not exist and that they are simply imagined by those who dare complain about them. Even if you highly disagree with my assertion, I invite you to try the session. After all, Reiki can do no harm, and you may find some amazing gifts happen as well by engaging this work.

Begin the session by creating your own Reiki Temple of Divine Light as shown in Chapter Twelve. Once that is created, continue as follows:

> *I invite my Reiki crystal to create a Reiki Sphere of Divine Gender around (name of person). I ask that this remain in place for the entire session.*

Add a deeper level of emotional safety by invoking the Reiki Sanctuary as follows:

> *I invite my Reiki crystal to create a Reiki Sanctuary around (name of person). I ask that this remain in place for the entire session.*

Follow this by asking your Reiki crystal to open a Reiki portal to the angelic realm, six inches above, as follows:

> *I invite my Reiki crystal to create a Reiki portal to the angelic realm (specify particular angel if you wish) six inches above (name of person's) crown chakra. I ask that this remain in place for the entire session.*

Follow this by asking your Reiki crystal to create a Reiki hologram of the archangel Raphael with his hands on the shoulders of the person being treated, as follows:

> *I invite my Reiki crystal to create a Reiki hologram of the archangel Raphael with his hands on (name of person's) shoulders for comfort and healing. I ask that this remain in place for the entire session.*

Once these initial steps of the session are fully in place, ask your Reiki crystal to create a Reiki meditation to compassionately reveal any gender bias that is held at a subconscious level:

> *I invite my Reiki crystal to bring (name of person) into a Reiki meditation to reveal all negative social conditioning about gender so that it can be witnessed and released. I ask that this remain in place for the next twenty minutes.*

Follow this by asking your Reiki crystal to create Reiki cords through the brain and nervous system to clear any negative social conditioning with regards to gender:

I invite my Reiki crystal to create a Reiki cord through (name of person's) brain and nervous system from the present moment backwards in time to the moment of their birth, to clear and release all negative gender beliefs, negative gender belief systems, and negative gender thought forms. I ask that this remain in place for the next twenty minutes.

Continue layering this session by asking your Reiki crystal to create Reiki holograms of the brain and nervous system free from any negative social conditioning with regards to gender:

I invite my Reiki crystal to create Reiki holograms of (name of person's) brain and nervous system free from all negative social conditioning about gender and to infuse this Reiki hologram into their brain and nervous system. I ask that this remain in place for as long as is for the highest good.

Continue deepening the layering process by asking your Reiki crystal to send Reiki to the mental body to clear and release any negative conditioning about gender:

I invite my Reiki crystal to send Reiki to (name of person's) mental body to release all negative social conditioning about gender. I ask that this continue for the next twenty minutes.

Further deepen this layering process by asking your Reiki crystal to bring all cells in that person's body that are holding gender trauma into a Reiki meditation, so that the consciousness of each cell emanates perfect health and is free from all gender trauma, as follows:

> *I invite my Reiki crystal to bring the consciousness in each cell holding gender trauma in (name of person's) body into a Reiki meditation to emanate a state of perfect health and know freedom from all gender trauma. I ask that this continue for the next twenty minutes.*

Now address any negative gender conditioning held at the karmic level by invoking the following:

> *I invite my Reiki crystal to create Lotus Reiki cords through (name of person's) karmic body from the present moment in time backwards to the moment of (name of person's) first incarnation. I ask that this remain in place for the next five minutes.*

I would not recommend leaving these cords in place for longer than five minutes since the level of release for some people can be quite extreme if left for too long. While the Reiki cords are still in place, invoke the following:

> *I invite my Reiki crystal to send Lotus Reiki to (name of person's) karmic body to release all negative karmic*

131

conditioning related to gender. I ask that this remain in place for the next twenty minutes.

Deepen the session even more by continuing to layer in more techniques simultaneously while Reiki is still flowing through all these. Invoke the following:

I invite my Reiki crystal to create a Reiki portal to the Divine inside of (name of person's) spine and karmic body. I ask that this Reiki portal remain in place for the next twenty minutes.

Continue to deepen the session with more layering techniques. Invoke the following:

I invite my Reiki crystal to create a Reiki hologram of (name of person's) karmic body free from any karmic issues related to gender, and to infuse this Reiki hologram into (name of person's) karmic body now. I ask that this Reiki hologram remain for as long as is for the highest good.

After five minutes, release all Reiki cords but allow the remaining functions to continue, as follows:

I ask my Reiki crystal to release all Reiki cords through (name of person's) karmic body.

Immediately follow by saying:

> *I invite my Reiki crystal to create a Reiki sieve and move it through (name of person's) karmic body from the moment of (name of person's) first incarnation through all of their lifetimes up to the present moment, lifting all energetic debris up sixty feet above me (or other person) and back to the Divine where it is fully transformed and released.*

Once the Reiki cords are released and the Reiki sieve has removed all related energetic debris, allow the remaining layered Reiki session to run unaltered for the next fifteen minutes. Then, begin to bring the session to a close with the following:

> *I invite my Reiki crystal to shift all the lines of light that it has been sending to now be for the most gentle and most perfect form of integration. I ask for this now.*

Then add to this process by using the following techniques to bring the session to an even gentler and more pleasant closure:

> *I invite my Reiki crystal to create a Reiki grounding cord from (name of person's) root chakra all the way down to the center of the Earth. I ask that this remain in place until it is no longer needed.*

Follow this by asking your Reiki crystal to create Reiki holograms of something pleasant, such as flowers, covering the recipient's body from head to toe:

> *I invite my Reiki crystal to create Reiki holograms of a thousand lilacs covering (name of person) from head to toe. I ask that these remain in place until they are no longer needed.*

The Reiki crystal will usually bring the Reiki integration process to a close within five minutes. The exact amount of time it takes depends on the person's energy system and how deep the session was. Once you sense the session is complete, invite the person being healed to drink plenty of water to assist in further release of any toxins that may have been moved out at the cellular level by the session.

The advanced Psychic Reiki sessions listed above are only suggestions and are not intended to limit you. If anything, they are meant to show you the depth of what is possible in a single Psychic Reiki session. Use them as you wish, and feel free to create your own advanced Psychic Reiki sessions based on your intuitive wisdom after working with all the Psychic Reiki tools in the previous chapters.

CHAPTER NINETEEN

Psychic Reiki and Psychic Readings

My journey as an energy healer began around the same time as my journey into esoteric arts, including divination through tarot, runes, and other means. I was very lucky to have some wonderful teachers in my training as a psychic and tarot reader. What they taught me was not just about the importance of learning how to train my own brain how to go into an alpha wave to enhance psychic ability, but also the importance of how to hold space when giving difficult psychic information to someone. Accuracy is just part of the equation of being a good reader. There are also the ethics of what to read, when to read, and how to deliver information in a way that is empowering to others as opposed to creating fear or harm. This is rarely, if ever, covered in a traditional Reiki training, or in many other energy healing trainings. Yet, there are many times when energy healers assume that being trained in Reiki or some other modality makes you an instant and well-trained psychic. It does not. And I have witnessed many gifted energy healers actually do harm by straying into the realm of psychic reading without the proper training.

When I began writing this book I struggled with the term Psychic Reiki because of this very issue. Yet that is what my guidance was telling me to title the book. Since the energy of Reiki can be accessed psychically through the Reiki crystal, the title for the book is the most accurate one. However, it is possible to blend the two worlds of energy healing and psychic readings as long as one is properly trained to do so. I have had the good grace of experiencing a few psychics who were also wonderful energy healers, and when integrated appropriately this can be a powerful combination. Here are some tips on what to do and not to do, and how to deepen your path as a psychic when it comes to energy healing. Please know these are just tips, not a full training in how to be a good psychic, something I believe needs to happen in person.

First, know that when giving an energy healing it is very common that you might get subtle or not-so-subtle messages while the healing is happening. In some cases that might be a spirit guide giving you information, or you may see colors, of have an empathetic reaction in your own body while the session is being performed on someone else. Lots of things can happen, and lots of times it might actually be a message from spirit. But know that is not always the case.

If you are getting a message that you believe is psychic during an energy healing, first tune in deeper and ask yourself if this is really about the other person or actually about you. Often, we can get triggered deeply by the issues we are helping to release in another person that are similar to our own. So, ask if this is really about them or if it is about you. If you keep getting a yes, that it is about the other person, then follow up at the end of the session by letting them know that some information came to you during the session. Ask if they would like to hear it. If they say no, respect that decision. If they say yes, know that you have actually already empowered them by asking for their consent to hear what information you have received.

Convey the information in a neutral and uncharged manner that also offers choices for the person whom you are sharing the psychic information with. Choice is the key. If, for example, you are sensing that someone is ill because they don't drink enough water or get enough nutrients in their diet, do not say something like: *You are sick because you don't eat right*. Instead say something like: *I sense that you would be empowered by paying more attention to your diet and being well hydrated*. The key is in both giving a positive choice as well as stating the phrase in a way that holds some form of empowerment for the individual. When performing an energy healing you can get many messages. Know that as an energy healer you are in a position of authority when giving the healing, so anything you say is going to carry some weight for the person receiving the healing. My own personal rule is not to share anything with the person unless spirit is truly hammering at me to do so, and even then I first ask the person if they actually want to hear what I sense.

I have heard of energy healers giving people highly inappropriate psychic readings and intuitive insights outside the context of a session. Blurting out unrequested information in public, or without the consent of the person in advance, displays poor judgment on the part of the reader, and often comes more from the ego of the person offering the unwanted information as they try to demonstrate to the world how psychic they are. My hard and fast rule is not to offer psychic readings when they are not requested.

Here are my five rules about infusing psychic readings into energy healings:

1. Ask first if this information is about them or actually about you.
2. Ask the person if they want to hear what you are sensing.
3. Make sure you convey all information in a way that is without an emotional charge and holds an element of choice for the person.
4. Be as positive and as empowering as possible.
5. Know that even if you are right ninety percent of the time as a psychic, you will be wrong ten percent of

the time. Treat each person as being potentially one of those ten percent.

If you truly feel you have a psychic gift, it is most likely in your best interest to get professionally trained as a psychic. A few things you might want to consider in the meantime, to test your Reiki psychic ability, include sending Reiki forward in time to your day in the morning before you leave your house. Write your intuitive impressions about your day down before you leave the house. When you come home at night, see if your psychic hits about the day were correct. Do this for a month. If you are one-hundred percent accurate all the time, reflect on how you wrote about each of those days. Did you write it in a way that was empowering to yourself? Recognize those times when you were conveying information in a way that was negative or reinforcing a negative prediction. Did you acknowledge in your writing that free will could always opt out of any future path, as long as one is willing to do the real work?

You may have a psychic gift that is real and worth developing. And, many of you will. There are few things as wonderful as a well-trained energy healer offering empowering psychic tidbits during a healing. But know it needs to be real and authentic. The work of the Reiki crystal can give you a head start in developing your psychic awareness, as can the practice of sending Reiki into the future and writing about what you sense to test your accuracy. Reiki meditations using the Reiki crystal are themselves also a kind of psychic development. Yet it is important to keep this in perspective. Reiki is not about us, our personalities, or our egos. Being a clear channel as a healer and a psychic is another key. The best psychics are ones that work hard to know their own energetic boundaries, to release the need to be seen as right, to surrender their own judgments and fear to the Divine. Reading this book and this chapter is not a guarantee of becoming a psychic energy healer, but it might be the first step for some.

CHAPTER TWENTY

Mikao Usui's Five Principles of Reiki and the Psychic Reiki Code of Ethics

Mikao Usui, the founder of Reiki, gave his students the Five Principles of Reiki to live by, which I encourage all students of Psychic Reiki to live by as well. These principles offer spiritual direction on how to act and how to be. Though often adapted by many Reiki masters, myself included, these five principles hold a core teaching as to how our actions shape us.

Mikao Usui's Five Principles of Reiki

Just for today, do not anger

Just for today, do not worry

Just for today, be grateful
Just for today, work honestly
Just for today, be kind to every living thing

Just for today are the first three words of each principle, reminding us that being in the moment, being here and now, is all we have control over. From there, each principle arises and can be harnessed as a form of spiritual guidance.

The first principle says *do not anger*. I was first exposed to these principles when I received my first degree training back in 1992, and, to be quite honest, I had a very hard time with the first one. It isn't because I think I am an angry person, but because in my own healing process discovering how much anger existed inside of me as a reaction to deep childhood trauma was a key to my healing and moving away from abusive situations that I had previously endured. My anger was my liberator, and took me out of places of abuse. So being told to not be angry simply didn't sit right with me. In my own evolution as a healer—now more than twenty years into my path as a Reiki master—I can hold that place of both respecting where I was, my own need to embrace all my feelings, and yet also hold space for these principles without having to adapt or rewrite them. I don't believe that Mikao Usui was saying to ignore anger, stuff it inside, and pretend it isn't there. But, instead, he was saying to not live from a place of anger. The beauty of Reiki is that it, along with other energy healing modalities I have worked with, healed my anger at its source. I no longer feel that anger, even when remembering some of the awful things I experienced as a child. So, today, I can live that principle fully. Still, I try to be very clear when teaching others that this principle was a challenge for me. Sometimes I can see some of my students are struggling with issues similar to the ones I had when being first initiated into Reiki, so I hold a place of openness to accept their anger, while not having to discard the principle itself. In Psychic Reiki you can also use your Reiki crystal to bring you into a Reiki meditation about this principle, and ask the Reiki crystal to show you how to heal, release, and transform issues of anger that still exist for you.

The second principle says *do not worry*. In the beautiful film *What About Me* by One Giant Leap the spiritual teacher Bhagavan Das says, "Worrying is praying for what you don't want. Stop praying for what you don't want." Not only does worry at times help manifest exactly what we want to avoid, but it simply isn't good for a person's mental, emotional, or physical wellbeing. Yet much of our mental and emotional energy can be taken up by worrying. Taking positive action in a situation is one of the best ways to remedy worry. But, you can also use your Reiki crystal to clear old patterns of worry from your mental body. Also, I recommend using your Reiki crystal to bring you into a Reiki meditation on this principle. When I do this for myself I sense a profound reminder of the level of Divine grace that exists in all situations, if we can only be wise enough to see it and honor it. That too is a wonderful remedy for worry.

Usui's third principle tells us to *be grateful*. Gratitude, counting our blessings, and being thankful are ways we remind the universe of our appreciation for the many gifts that happen daily through the miracle of being alive. Keeping a gratitude or blessing journal is one technique you can use to be in alignment with this important Reiki principle. Also, you can make a daily practice of repeating the following: *"Today I am grateful for (fill in the blank)."* Practice that for several minutes each day. Doing so can radically change your life. And, as with the previous principles, you can also go deeper by inviting your Reiki crystal to take you into a Reiki meditation about Usui's principle of being grateful.

The fourth Reiki principle tells us to *work honestly*. What does it mean to work honestly? For me, personally, it means showing up, being present, working hard, and doing the best I can in any job that I do, while also not stealing from anyone or misrepresenting myself in any way. One might also infer that working honestly also means not gouging others with ridiculously high fees for workshops and healings—something that still happens all too often in the world of Reiki and other forms of energy healing. To really honor this principle the important thing is to be honest with yourself; do a fearless inventory of yourself in how you show up in your work. You can do that as a regular written exercise for yourself, and also take it even deeper by making it a regular practice to have your Reiki crystal bring you into a Reiki meditation on the principle of *work honestly*.

Mikao Usui's fifth Reiki principle says *be kind to every living thing.* That principle relates to the concept of *ahimsa,* the Sanskrit term for "do no harm," which is a major tenet in the religions of Hinduism, Jainism, and Buddhism. However, Usui's fifth Reiki principle takes that concept of ahimsa a step further into the realm kindness. Being kind is more than just avoiding harming others. Being kind is having an open and generous heart, and making choices that benefit not only your own spiritual journey but also the whole, the greater community of sentient beings. One of the best ways to be kind to others is to raise your overall level of awareness, to see other beings as they truly are, to acknowledge, as Dr. Martin Luther King Jr. said, "All are caught in an inescapable network of mutuality." The best way to embody this principle is to constantly work on yourself. By releasing your fears, prejudices, your old traumas, negative thought patterns and conditioning you make the vessel of your being more open to the expansive state of being from which authentic kindness can emerge. There is no one quick and easy solution to engage this principle, as it is an ongoing practice. You can begin by first being kind to yourself, try to extend yourself to others when appropriate. Also, as before, use Reiki crystal meditations to deepen your connection with this principle. Naturally, you can ask your Reiki crystal to bring you into a Reiki mediation on the principle itself. Also, you can also invite your Reiki crystal to reveal to you your own blind spots to being kind, your own areas you need the most work on. Make this an ongoing practice and it will deepen your own spiritual path enormously.

The Psychic Reiki Code of Ethics has its foundation in Mikao Usui's Reiki principles, and is not meant or intended to replace those principles. I have found over the years of teaching energy healing that technique is not enough, and that a good moral compass is often left out of many trainings related to energy work and energy healing. This code of ethics is intended to address common errors I have witnessed among Reiki practitioners and other energy healers:

Psychic Reiki Practitioner Code of Ethics

1. I live and abide my Mikao Usui's Five Principles of Reiki without judging or condemning those Reiki practitioners who ignore or have issues with those principles.
2. I honor the free will of other beings and their evolutionary process, and thus do not send energy healing to any individual without their consent.
3. I refrain from any form of sexual relationships with any clients or students.
4. I honor the sacred space of an energy healing, as well as vulnerability of anyone in my care during a healing, including the moments immediately before and after, by refraining from any type of self-promotional language, sales language, or other activity that might consciously

or unconsciously take advantage of my position and power as a healer.

5. I acknowledge as a Psychic Reiki teacher that students often have powerful ideas that can influence me and help my evolution as a teacher. I acknowledge and credit those students and their ideas whenever possible, and refuse to take ownership of any ideas or concepts that are not my own.

6. I make my classes and healings affordable so that the circle of light grows far and wide.

7. I acknowledge there are many paths and ways to access Divine energy healing and that Reiki and Psychic Reiki techniques are but one path within a rainbow of many colors. I refrain from judging, disparaging, or engaging in an ego competition with teachers and students of other paths. I am welcoming of any form of light that brings healing to others and to the planet.

This code of ethics can and should be combined with Usui's Reiki principles as a guide for how to live and be in the world as a Psychic Reiki practitioner. I also recommend you, as a practitioner, take time to write your own energy healing manifesto, to take ownership of your own values and apply them to your energy healing practice.

CHAPTER TWENTY-ONE

Teaching Psychic Reiki

Teaching Psychic Reiki is easy. It is meant to be easy. The Reiki crystal you were empowered to through this book is meant to be shared. It is not meant to be hidden away as a secret for an enlightened few, but is intended as a tool for all who want to access it. To be a Psychic Reiki teacher all you need is a desire to share this work, and at least one willing student. However, this does not detract from the sense of awe and beauty that will come from sharing this work. It is simultaneously simple, yet also sacred and profound.

Empowering others to their own Reiki crystal does not involve any complex sequence of symbols, nor any intensive training. If you want to share this work with others, and have a person's consent, you can empower them simply by asking your Reiki crystal to empower that person to their own Reiki crystal. It is that easy. Below is the template for this request:

> *I invite my Reiki crystal to empower (name of person) to their own Reiki crystal.*

Once you have made the request, the Reiki crystal then begins sending a session that will usually last for approximately seven minutes, though I have seen it happen in as few as three minutes. What happens is that your Reiki crystal essentially creates a duplicate of itself in the other person's energy field. If that person's field is quite clear and not in need of much healing, the empowerment will take less time. If you are someone who is sensitive to energy healing, you might even sense the presence of the Reiki crystal in that person's energy field once it is fully formed.

Know that teaching Psychic Reiki to another person involves more than just the empowerment. Although it is not required to teach someone every technique in this book, you should show them how to do a Psychic Reiki session on themselves, as well as others, and also teach them how to perform a Reiki meditation using their Reiki crystal. That at least gives a person a real foundation in how to use this work to improve their life and the lives of others. The Reiki holograms, Reiki portals, and other advanced techniques in this book can be shared if appropriate and if time permits, but do not let that detract you from sharing the essential core of this work with as many willing students as you can.

Once you have empowered a person to their own Reiki crystal, teach the person to perform a basic Psychic Reiki self session. Talk them through each step, reminding them that they can activate Reiki to flow from their Reiki crystal simply through a mental or verbal request to their Reiki crystal. Use the Psychic Reiki self session protocol from Chapter 4 as a guide. Once the person has finished a Psychic Reiki self session, discuss their experience with them. Ask them what it felt like for them to be communicating with their own Reiki crystal. Discuss the self session for several minutes until you are convinced they feel comfortable with the concept of their Reiki crystal having Divine intelligence, and that they can activate Reiki simply through a mental or verbal request to their Reiki crystal. Those are the two most key elements for them to understand, as all else will flow naturally if those two key concepts are understood.

After the self session, ask the person to give a basic Psychic Reiki session to another person. If this is an individual, one-on-one-style training then you will most likely need to be that person receiving a Psychic Reiki session. Use the protocol from Chapter 5, guiding your student along each step. As you did before, ask them a few questions after the session is complete to again reinforce the key concepts of the Reiki crystal having Divine intelligence and that it will respond to a person's mental or verbal requests.

Now, begin sharing how to perform a Reiki meditation using the Reiki crystal. The evidence of Divine intelligence within the Reiki crystal will be more apparent once you begin teaching how to use the Reiki crystal to perform Reiki meditations. Often, this is when a deeper layer of excitement begins to be exhibited by the student (or students). Share some of the types of Reiki meditations shown in Chapter 6, as well as those Reiki meditations you may have created for yourself.

Once a student has a foundational knowledge of how to do a Psychic Reiki session on themselves and others, and how to send Psychic Reiki sessions distantly, it is up to your discretion as a teacher whether or not they are ready for the advanced Psychic Reiki techniques outlined in this book. If you feel that they are, proceed at a pace that works for the student. Some people need time with each tool to fully digest and integrate on an emotional level what it means to have their consciousness and awareness stretched to the levels of some Psychic Reiki tools. Others might adapt to those adjustments very easily and be able to assimilate the full range of tools in a few hours. Trust your judgment, as there is no one right way to do it. Just know you should rely on this book as the primary source with regards to any instruction you give related to Reiki holograms, Reiki portals, the Reiki crystal healing grid, and the other advanced techniques explored in this book. I also recommend making those students aware of this book, given it is the primary source text of this work. You don't need to supply it, but at least let them know it exists. Also, supply all students with handouts of Mikao Usui's Reiki principles as well as the Psychic Reiki code of ethics. Reiki is a journey, and by introducing others to at least the basics of Psychic Reiki you have helped them take the first step forward on a path of powerful spiritual transformation.

CHAPTER TWENTY-TWO

Planetary and Personal Time-Released Healings

All copies of this book, as has been demonstrated in previous chapters, have the ability to send Reiki energy healing. That does not have to be limited to the reader, but can also be for the world at large. What follows are exercises that program this book, and each copy of this book, to be consistently working for the betterment of humankind, the planet as a whole, and you as an individual.

This book is creating a Reiki portal to the Divine inside of the core of the Earth. If you wish, please join in this exercise by asking your own Reiki crystal to do the same. This Reiki portal will remain in place for as long as is for the highest good.

Every morning from nine o'clock to a quarter past nine this copy of this book is sending a Reiki energy clearing of the living space of the person who possesses this book, or to the bookstore in which it is being displayed if not yet purchased.

This copy of this book is sending Reiki daily from noon to 12:30 p.m. to shift human consciousness to live in true alignment with our planet and environment, for the betterment of all beings. Just for today, if you wish, please join with this book, and any other participating Psychic Reiki practitioners, in this collective healing.

This book is creating a half hour long group Reiki meditation for all willing Psychic Reiki practitioners to join, daily at ten o'clock at night, wherever you are. This Reiki meditation is focused on visualizing world peace, which includes not only peace between nations but also peace between races, genders, and peace between humanity and all other life forms. To participate in this meditation, simply intend to do so at ten o'clock on any night you wish. As this collective grows, so grows the awareness of peace in our collective consciousness as human beings.

Every night from eleven o'clock to half past eleven this book is sending Reiki to manifest peace by clearing the energetic signature of hatred from the Earth's energy field, and to transform that vibration into love. Just for today, if you wish, please join with this book, and any other participating Psychic Reiki practitioners, in this collective healing.

This book sends a Reiki energy healing tonight from three to four o'clock in the morning to anyone who has it placed under their bed or pillow.

As a thank you for guiding me to write this book, this book is creating a Reiki portal to the spirit of Neem Karoli Baba on the blank page following. May his presence be in this book always.

9 781939 681843